AMBLING THROUGH HAMPSHIRE BASINGSTOKE AND BEYOND

Thirty Circular Walks Around Hampshire Inns and Tea Shops

Malcolm Parker

Other publications in the series
"Pub Walks in Dorset"
"40 More Pub Walks in Dorset"
"Pub Walks in Hants & the IOW"
"Pub Walks in West Sussex"
"Pub Walks in East Sussex"
"Pub Walks in Kent"
"Pub Walks in Devon"
"Pub Walks in Cornwall"
"Pub Walks in the New Forest"
"Pub Walks in Somerset"
"Pub Walks in North Surrey"
"Pub Walks in South Surrey"
"40 More Pub Walks in Surrey"
"Dorset Teashop Walks"
"Pub Walks in Hardy's Wessex"
"Walks in the New Forest"
"Pub Walks Along the Dorset Coast"

© Malcolm Parker

Power Publications
1 Clayford Ave., Ferndown
Dorset BH22 9PQ
e-mail: sales@powerpublications.co.uk

ISBN 0951450271

Publisher's note
Whilst every care has been taken to ensure the accuracy of all the information given in this book, errors will occur due to many factors. Paths are sometimes rerouted, new stiles and gates are often erected and the pubs frequently change hands. Neither the printer nor the publishers can accept responsibility for any inaccuracies.

Front Cover: Castle of Comfort, Medstead
Back Cover: Coach and Horses, Rotherwick
Photographs: Malcolm Parker and Mike Power

First published February 2005
Printed by Pardy and Son (Printers) Ltd, Ringwood, Hants.

Introduction

Hello and welcome to my little book of walks in and around the town of Basingstoke. This part of England may not boast spectacular waterfalls and snow-capped peaks, but these are more than compensated for by beautiful churches, curvaceous downlands, crystal clear chalk streams and picturesque thatched cottages so I do hope you'll be pleasantly surprised by the abundance of aesthetic and historical pleasures to be found tucked away right on your doorstep.

Most of these walks offer tranquillity and a degree of solitude, but I make no apology for including a couple which in contrast barely leave tarmac or townscape. It's an inescapable fact that Basingstoke has rarely been celebrated for its charm and character, so I do hope the town walk in particular will open people's eyes to some beguiling corners and help to redress that. If you work or live in Basingstoke, I hope this book will reveal a few more insights about locations you may have heard of or pass every day and perhaps encourage you to delve further into aspects of Basingstoke's history.

Walking is one of the simplest, cheapest and most rewarding activities available and it's also extremely good for you. As most people have mastered its technical complexities by the age of two, I'll not bore you with intricacies, but if you want to know how long each walk will take you, work on averaging 2mph and you shouldn't be far out.

It has been known to rain occasionally in this country, so do check the weather forecast the day before and as even setting out on the brightest days, you may come across mud, rain, or both, a lightweight waterproof jacket and some comfortable walking shoes or waterproof trainers are recommended accessories as is a compass and stick to deal with long nettles.

All the walks are circular and suitable for anyone of reasonable fitness and they all have a pub or a teashop nearby where you can indulge in suitably restorative refreshment after your walk. It's sensible to book ahead for parties of six or more, try to share transport to tiny villages and please ask permission before filling a pub car park and not filling the pub! Alternative parking is shown where available.

All the establishments have been visited during the research for this book but as opening hours vary and establishments may change hands or close at short notice, I've given a contact number with each, so you can check for yourself on the day of your walk and prepare sandwiches if all has gone awry. All the routes are along public rights of way or permissive paths and although a sketch map accompanies each, you will find the appropriate Ordnance Survey map a useful accessory for identifying features I haven't noted.

Responsible Behaviour
Keep your dogs under control
Use gates or stiles where provided
Do not:
  Light or cause fires
  Do any damage
  Leave litter
  Leave gates open (unless they are clearly propped or fastened open)
  Disturb livestock, wildlife, or habitats

End of lecture, now get out there and enjoy yourself!

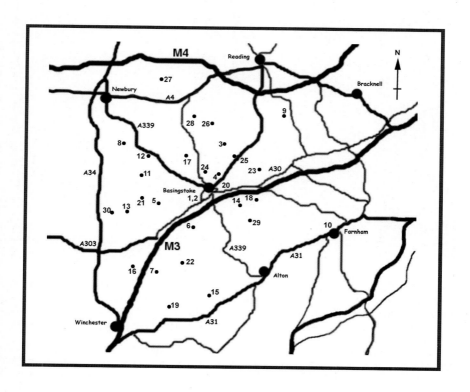

Dayers Bistro, Basingstoke

George Willis, a noted amateur archaeologist and historian who's collection of clocks and artefacts evolved to become the nearby Willis museum would be very pleased to see that his former watchmaking shop in Wote Street is now the home of what has recently been voted by readers of the local paper, Basingstoke's Favourite Sandwich Shop.

Dayers Bistro was opened in September 2001 by the brothers Simon and Chris Dayer alongside their colleague Dawn Valler. Chris, a chef who has worked with such luminaries as Marco Pierre White and who is described as the 'local Jamie Oliver' by some, defined the company policy of fresh, fresh food and value for money, virtues which will be found in every bite of their delicious concoctions.

Whether you're a simple soul who fancies one of their all day breakfasts, a more refined gourmet tempted by their Ciabatta crammed with Turkey, Stuffing, Sliced Sausage and Cranberry, or an altogether more exotic individual seduced by the Toasted Panini Palermo, with Smoked Salmon, Cream Cheese and Fresh Basil you will not be disappointed. As well as these items typical of their regular lunchtime menu, you'll also find numerous 'Specials of the day' chalked up on the blackboard. Dayers has a small seating area downstairs and a more capacious Bistro section upstairs and its open 07:30-16:30 Monday to Saturday (closed Sundays)

Telephone 01256 334747

Approx. distance of walk: 7 miles. Start at OS Map Ref SU 637518.

There is a pay-and-display car park near the bistro, this is free all day on Sundays, but it is restricted to a maximum of 3 hours Mondays to Saturdays. While this should be enough time to complete the walk and have a meal afterwards, you may want to park in the towns multi-story car park if you wish to take the walk at a more leisurely pace. Alternatively, on a sunny day you might prefer to take a picnic and some bread to feed the ducks and start your walk at the free car park next to the Black Dam Ponds where you can pick up the route at point 27.

Hampshire guidebooks have rarely been complementary about the market town of Basingstoke, writing it off as somewhere that you'd pass through but not want to stop even before WWII. The major town centre redevelopment in the 1960's was unsympathetic to say the least, and it's taken a very long process of gradual changes and improvements to warm Basingstoke's heart. Finally with the opening of the Festival Place shopping centre, the town has really started to come together as the smart, interesting place that its principals and its people have always wanted it to be. This walk takes you through Basingstoke old and new, revealing just a few of the facets that have made it what it is today. The majority of the route is along tarmac footpaths but suitable footwear is an advisable precaution to traverse the mud at point 22.

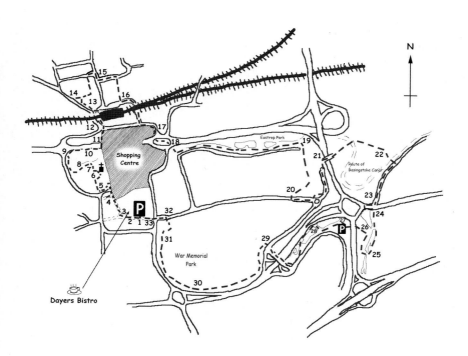

Walk No. 1

1. From the car park, make your way north along May Place alleyway next to the St Johns Ambulance building to emerge on London Street.

This street was the first part of the town to be pedestrianised in 1978 and its now quite difficult to believe that it was once the main road through Basingstoke from London to Winchester. The sculpture just in front of you here is entitled "The Family" by Mike Smith, and was erected in 1993.

2. We turn right along London Street, passing the attractive modern ironwork above and around the Rhu Bar on your left, which is one of the oldest buildings in the street. Also on the left we pass Drakes bar, with some rather cheerful Victorian brickwork and strange variations between the windows above. This building stands on the site of the 16th century Fleur-de-Lys, an inn where in 1645 Oliver Cromwell is reputed to have stayed for several nights at the end of the famous siege of Basing House.

3. Continuing along London Street we emerge into the Market Place, scene of weekly markets since the 13th century. The Willis Museum is here; housed in the Italianate building that was Basingstoke's Town Hall from 1832 to 1981. When first built, the ground floor was open and you could pass through the colonnades to market stalls beneath. To date no local dignitaries have admitted to modelling for the faces on the two ornamental urns above the entrance, but we know who they are. Directly opposite, behind what is now Barclays Bank stood a rather grim building known as the Assembly Rooms where Jane Austen attended dancing lessons and the occasional Ball in the 1790's. The older part of the bank here has some wonderful Art Nouveau airbricks.

4. Turn right now along Church Street we proceed down into the valley of the Loddon where you'll find extraordinarily consistent weather according to the readings on the Museums illuminating weather panel – that is unless they've finally been repaired! Halfway down the hill Longleys has a wonderful old frontage with a particularly swoopy door handle and an old enamel sign just inside the window that once graced another shop opposite. At the bottom of the hill, just before you go up and over the footbridge we find Cross Street on our left, which with its fine selection of 17th and 18th century buildings is worthy of further examination. Here set into the pavement you'll find hand carved sandstone panels installed in 1992 which celebrate five distinct themes, some directly linked to Basingstoke and others rather more abstract. If it's sunny, stand at the foot of the sundial and your shadow should point out the time.

5. Returning to Church Street, cross the footbridge and on the other side immediately turn left and then left again to follow the path just before the building.

Where the path turns sharply right by the wall, we enter Church Lane, an ancient 'lawe path' which prior to the towns redevelopment was a narrow alley weaving between tight packed houses all the way back up to Cross Street. There is a good view here across to one of Basingstoke's few encounters with Art Deco, a building known as Queens Parade, which was built in 1933.

6. We pause for a moment when we reach the end of Church Lane. The bungalows and gardens you see here are built upon the site of a devastating bombing raid that took place in 1940, killing several people and destroying many homes. Turn right here, crossing the square where it opens out to bring us to the front of St Michael's Church. Although a church has stood on this spot for almost 1000 years, most of the current Perpendicular building dates from the Tudor period. That it remains largely unaltered is quite remarkable when one considers some its history, not only surviving those German bombs which blew out all of it's windows bar one, but also a major fire in the 1930's that destroyed most of the roof and an internal explosion during the Civil War while it was being used as a stables and ammunition store. Damage to the stonework from Civil War musket shots peppers the outside of the south wall and was supplemented by scars from flying shrapnel from the bombs in WWII. The small chapel on the southeast corner with its Tudor chimney is thought to be the oldest part, possibly 14th century and the redundant arch you can see above its roof shows how it only narrowly escaped the main rebuilding which took place in the 1520's. There are some excellent gargoyles, particularly around the unusual two-storied porch, which dates from 1539 and which lost most of the statue in the recess above the door thanks to Cromwell's puritan troops. The sundial only works occasionally now due to foliage in the works. Thomas Hardy obliquely refers to St Michael's as "gaunt and unattractive" in

one of his Wessex tales and while I'm not pushed on that flint and stone chequer work on the North side, I think overall he was a little harsh!

7. Proceed to the entrance to the church car park near to St Michael's porch. Across the tarmac in front of you will see Church Cottage, the town's most important surviving timber-framed house. Built shortly after the church, it was originally the Priest's House and the large Barn to the rear is where the tithes for the parish were collected. Ancient corn from this time trapped in the mortise joints was revealed when the building was being restored in the 1970's. In Victorian times the building became a school and to the right of the porch can be seen the deep grooves in the wall made by children sharpening their slate pencils.

8. Pick up the narrow path, which runs by the wall to the left of the Church Office and you will emerge in Glebe Gardens. In the past known rather less romantically as Sheep Wash Meadow, this pretty spot was once the formal gardens of what is now known as Chute House over in the northeast corner. This was the parsonage for St Michael's from Georgian times until the 1960's and was the birthplace of Thomas Warton, son of the local vicar, professor of poetry at Oxford from 1757 to 1767 and Poet Laureate from 1785 until his death five years later. He was no Betjeman, and was apparently a rather aromatic gentleman who never let personal hygiene get in the way of other matters. He is perhaps better celebrated for his History of English Poetry and as a noble editor of The Oxford Sausage than for any of the rather dull and pompous compositions he produced during his laureateship.

Stay on the tarmac path and turn left just before you come to the bridge, following this path alongside one of the few open stretches of the River Loddon within Basingstoke.

9. At the next junction in the path, we turn right and then right again to skirt the western edge of the gardens. To your left prominent on the skyline is the grand white edifice of the manufacturing plant built for the pharmaceutical firm Eli Lilly in 1939. It was such a landmark that it had to be camouflaged during the war to prevent German bombers using it as a reference point. As we come to the northwest corner of the gardens, turn left toward the subway and take the pathway just before it off to the right.

10. As you turn the corner, look up to face the distinctive architecture of The Anvil, Basingstoke's marvellous concert-hall building. It was built in 1994 on the site of what was for over 200 years May's Brewery, one of Basingstoke's most important companies during the Victorian era, a time when Hampshire was one of the principle hopgrowing districts in the country. Glebe Farm further along the path on your right remains to bear testament to the importance of agriculture in Basingstoke's still very recent past.

11. Continuing along the footpath we return once more to Church Street where in the 13th century the Hospital of St John stood on the opposite side of the road. As pretty much all trace of this had disappeared as long ago as 1700, only a few of today's residents remember it. Today, before we cross over, look right and you'll see 'The Great Wall', an unbroken vista of unimaginative brickwork symbolically portrayed in a 1970's TV documentary as the "antithesis of creative urban development in the UK". I don't know about that, but the perspective does remain a worthy testament to the occasional failings of architects to see their designs from the viewpoint of the man in the street!

12. Cross over and turn left to cross the footbridge toward the Anvil. Continue straight on past the entrance then follow the curving steps to the left. At the top of these stairs, you'll see a lovely little statue called 'Poppy' directly ahead of you. Designed by Tom Merrifield, this privately commissioned work proved so popular when it appeared in the local paper that a public campaign led to its purchase and installation. Turn left now and cross the Alencon Link road - named after the French Town 'twinned' with Basingstoke in the 1970's. On the other side, we take the raised path to the right under the railway bridge. This road was lined with old houses on both sides until the 1960's redevelopment and on the left parapet of the bridge can still be seen the outline of the roof of Soper's Almshouses which stood in that spot from the 1890's.

13. Having passed under the railway, we now turn immediately right and take the stairs up and over the footbridge, pausing to look over to the far side of platform 1 which was the departure point for trains along the famous Basingstoke & Alton Light Railway. On the other side of the bridge, you enter one of Basingstoke's more historic sites, the medieval burial ground commonly known as

the Liten – a tasteful corruption of the Anglo-Saxon word for Corpse-ground. Follow the path to the left and you see before you the remains of two separate buildings.

The hexagonal tower and arches are the remains of the Guild Chapel of the Holy Trinity, erected at the same time as St Michaels Church by local nobleman and friend of Henry VIII Lord Sandys, as a burial chapel for his family. One of the priests of this chapel was Charles Butler whose work 'Histori of Bee's' in 1609 was much celebrated for giving the musical notes that Bees hum while swarming.

Behind the Trinity chapel over to the left are the remains of the square tower of much earlier Chapel of the Holy Ghost, said to have been a magnificent building comparable to Canterbury albeit to a slightly more modest scale. Erected shortly after the Liten was established, this was in ruins by the time that the Trinity Chapel was added and the remaining section stands only thanks to its conversion to a rectangular schoolroom in 1635. By that time, the Trinity chapel was also neglected and in decay, a process quickly hastened by Oliver Cromwell's troops. About a hundred years later, when the famous naturalist Gilbert White of Selbourne was a pupil, the Liten had become the school playground, and it was a favourite amusement of the boys to undermine and topple sections of the Trinity chapel wall – who said vandalism was a modern phenomenon! The two notable tombs with carved effigies within the chapel walls are not in their original locations having been buried in ancient times and uncovered in 1817. The mutilated Knightly figure is believed to be Sir William de Brayboef, Lord of the manor of Eastrop who died in 1283, the other tomb is of an unknown civilian.

14. Continue up the hill, now decoratively paved with long fallen tombstones. At the top, take the path sloping down to the left. This brings you to a fabulous Victorian gothic lodge whose splendid over-the-top architecture was once mirrored by two towering chapels 80 feet high back up in the cemetery, built when it was enlarged and reopened for customers in 1858. Sadly these chapels had to be demolished in the 1950's when the cost of maintaining them far outweighed their usage. The little lodge house was the birthplace of Basingstoke's most famous son in modern times, journalist and cricket commentator John Arlott OBE.

15. Return to the top of the slope and continue straight on along the main path. At the junction with the gardeners shed, turn left. The path here leads us up to Burgess Road where we turn right. Proceed along to the junction with Vyne Road and turn right again. Down the hill a few yards, we then cross over into Soper Grove.

16. Strolling past the mannerly Victorian villas, turn right opposite Fencott Place to follow the narrow path which runs to the right of the garages. This is the course of an old footpath that once led north from the town all the way to Sherborne St John. We follow this alleyway back down towards the town passing the car park on your right, the site of Basingstoke's Cattle Market from Victorian times until the 1960's. When you reach the road, turn left down the hill, and follow the road around to the right to go under the railway bridge and into Bunnian Place. You might spot the forgivable misspelling on the railway bridge, it's almost certain this road wasn't named after the author John Bunyan, but rather Alderman Thomas Bunney who owned several properties in the area when the road was first established.

17. The Queen's Arms is the only building here to escape redevelopment in the 1960's and it's very much the last outpost before we confront the modern town. We continue down Bunnian Place to rejoin the Alencon Link. Cross the road here and then turn left down the hill, as you round the bend, you are greeted with an uncompromising view of modern Basingstoke. The imposing frontage of Churchill Plaza towers to your right; over to your left there is the mirrored curvature of the Sun Life offices while straight ahead glows one of the illuminated pinnacles of Festival Place.

18. Continue on down through the subway and you emerge in the middle of Eastrop Roundabout. It's almost impossible to believe from today's scene that until the 1920's you'd see before you a tranquil tree-lined spot popular with anglers where Eastrop Bridge crossed the final stretch of the Basingstoke Canal. Turn left and follow the path to take the subway to the right. On the other side, continue across the small plaza where fountains echo the Loddon beneath cross the car park exit road then take the path off to the left, which leads us into Eastrop Park.

19. Following the red path alongside the channelled River Loddon, we can enjoy the fine variety of trees and in summer months

the beautifully maintained ornamental flowerbeds. Continue along the red path, past the boating ponds, the Boat House and the children's play area. As you approach the end of the park, a path leads down to a small footbridge on your left. We actually take the path in the opposite direction passing through a screen of tall Hawthorns, which were part of the original Basingstoke Canal Hedgerow planted in 1805 along its northern bank. Here turn right and then quickly left to take the red and black path leading up the hill to the left of the children's playground.

20. This path follows the route of an old cart track known as Deadman's Lane; nothing as far as I could establish to do with shuffling off mortal coils, but simply a dead end lane down to a small wharf on the canal. Follow this path up the hill, cross straight over when you come to the small road called The Rushes and continue along the path. At the end, we rejoin the old London Road, where we cross over and turn left to pass the recently restored Milestone placed there sometime after this road became a turnpike in 1736. Walk down the hill and cross back over London Road where you see the footpath on the left.

21. Follow this down to the junction and turn left along Barbel Avenue. Cross at the end of this path into Acorn Close and follow the path to the right of the houses. Where the path divides, bear right to turn up and over the footbridge. Here we cross the A339, the gateway to Basingstoke, a scene dominated to the north by Fanum House, the AA's temple to the motorist, opened by the Queen in 1972.

22. On the other side of the bridge, continue down the muddy path until you come to a junction with another path in the trees from your left, here we again cross the route of the old Basingstoke canal. Carry straight on past the Basingstoke Canal Heritage Footpath sign and we come out onto the floodplains and water meadows of the river Loddon known as Basing Fen. Crossing this open peat moor, bear diagonally to the right to pick up a narrower path leading to a gap in the hedge marked with a marker post. A few yards further on walk along the duckboard's over the marshland crossing another of the crystal-clear tributaries of the Loddon at the end. Pass through the metal kissing gate where we again cross the route of the canal and turn right along Redbridge Lane.

23. Immediately on your right, we pass Swing Bridge Cottages; built in the 1840's and named rather aptly after a swing bridge across the canal, which our path from Basing Fen would once have crossed. Several hundred yards further down Redbridge Lane, we pass the remains of Upper Mill on the right, one of two corn mills near Basingstoke that took their power from the River Loddon. Behind the mill site, the pure spring waters have provided an ideal spot for watercress beds. Cross over to left hand side of the road where we enter the one-way section until you reach the junction with the A30.

24. Traffic passes this point at high speed in both directions, so instead of getting yourself killed trying to sprint across, turn right down the hill for 100 yards and make your way across at the roundabout where it's easy to do it in relative safety! Once right across on the far side, turn left back up the A30 until you are back opposite Redbridge Lane. Here we turn right onto the path beside the large metal gate, which takes us down toward the Hampshire Wildlife Trust's nature reserve.

25. At the junction with other paths, ignore the gravelled path straight ahead and turn left onto Basingstoke Common. Follow the hedgerow on your right along the bottom of the field and after a few hundred yards; you will come to a large path, which we follow into the woods passing between the two old fishponds known as the Pipes. These originally supplied both fish and fresh water to Hackwood House on the other side of the M3. On the other side of the ponds follow the path round to the right - in the summer the clearing on the corner is a spectacular Wildflower meadow created by local schoolchildren. Continue round to the right and turn off the main path to explore the wildlife along the wooden platforms. Follow these all the way to the end where steps return you to the tarmac path.

26. Go right and then turn left at the junction to follow a path under the subway where you emerge at Black Dam Ponds car park.

27. Take the tarmac path that curves in front of the main pond. The ponds as we see them today were created in 1969, but this area was originally dammed to control flooding and also to provide a consistent supply to the Mill that we passed earlier. This area is a favourite spot for local people to feed the Coots, Swans, Mallards and Moorhens that

gather here in flocks and it's also a good place to spot migratory birds in the autumn.

28. Continue along the path, turning right at the junction with the thinner tarmac path. Follow this round through some lovely woodland. Continue straight on over the little wooden footbridge, and this brings you back to the main footpath. Here go right and then right again at the end up and over the road bridge.

29. On the other side of the bridge, turn right to take the subway under Old Common Road and then walk up the steps. At the top turn left and follow this tarmac path, continue straight at the junction with other paths to pass the Tennis Centre on the right.

30. Continuing along, the formal hedge on the right marks the entrance to the War Memorial Park, purchased by public subscription in 1921. This was originally known as Goldings Park when it was established in the 18th century as the grounds of a private residence. Take the path to the right where you come to the gap in the wall and follow the main path to the left of the children's playground. If you keep your eyes peeled along here, there are some lovely passages of poetry to spot, which were set into the path in 1995.

31. Keep left and follow the main path round towards the bandstand. This was built in 1901, and was originally erected in what was then Basingstoke's main park at Fairfield's further to the southwest, moving here when the Memorial Park was inaugurated. Further along the path we come to the aviary where the twitterings of the Budgies and Zebra Finches are always a great attraction for small children. Continue along the main path; turn left when you reach the gates and head towards the war memorial. The ditch you cross is an original haha, dating back to the parks origins as private land. Haha's were aesthetic alternatives to fences used to prevent livestock from getting into formal gardens without spoiling the view. On your left, you now pass Goldings, the fine Georgian house after which the park was originally named. No longer a private residence, it now forms part of the municipal offices and is a popular location for weddings. It contains the only substantially unaltered Georgian interior in the town.

32. Passing by the war memorial, we come again to London Road where we turn left back up towards the town centre. Ahead of you, you'll see the rather controversial Triumphal Gates, which were installed in

1992 'heralding' the entrance to the town centre. Personally I think they'd work better a little further down London Street, but you judge for yourself!

33. Cross straight over at the traffic lights to re-enter pedestrianised London Street. On your left, you'll see the historic Deane's Almshouses. These were founded in 1608 by Sir James Deane with money left to him by the person who is probably Basingstoke's most illustrious and wealthiest son – Sir James Lancaster, one of Queen Elizabeth I's leading sea captains and founder of the East India Trading Company. The homes were built to house eight poor widows and are still used for that purpose today although I'm told they're rather nicer to look at than they are to live in. Thankfully the pig market that was rather tactlessly installed in front of them has long gone and they were all modernised and extended to the rear in the 1960's. Continue along London Street to the Market Square and you will find Dayers on the right down Wote Street, to the right of the museum.

The Golden Lion, Basingstoke

The thatched cottage that was the original Lion public house, still stands opposite The Golden Lion, built as a much-needed replacement to accommodate an ever-growing volume of post war customers that came as traffic grew at this once important crossroads along the Basingstoke bypass. Today both buildings still stand in the same location but this is a much more tranquil spot, with the Basingstoke bypass itself bypassed by the M3 and the old Cliddesden road now closed to traffic at both ends.

The pub is now a popular haunt for office workers from the nearby trading estate and current tenants of this Scottish and Newcastle House, Angela and Mark McBride were busy decorating the lounge bar at the time of my visit to complete a thorough refurbishment.

The menu is filling and wholesome rather than flamboyant, but there is excellent fare for the hungry walker whose thirst will also be slaked by such fine ales as Courage Best, London Pride or Hogs Back Tea, a particularly popular beverage with the local drollery.

The pub is open 11:00-23:00 Monday to Friday, 11:30-23:00 Saturday and 12:00-22:30 Sunday with food available 11:30-22:00 Monday to Friday, 12:00-22:00 Saturday and 12:00-21:30 Sunday.

The telephone number is 01256 464699. Dogs are welcome in the public bar; the licence position regarding children is currently under review.

Walk No. 2

The pub is situated next to the Golden Lion roundabout, along The Harrow Way/ Grove Road.

Approx. distance of walk: 7 miles. Start at OS Map Ref SU 638505.

Parking is available along Viables Lane, along the section of old road directly alongside the pub or if you're using the pub, in the pub car park.

This walk is not suitable for young children due to the difficult crossing of the A339 at point 7 although you could of course split the walk into two and return along the same path. This walk takes in two notable parts of Basingstoke history following a small section of The Basingstoke & Alton Light Railway on its way out into the countryside and then returning to glimpse just a fragment of the glories that make up the Hackwood Park Estate on your return.

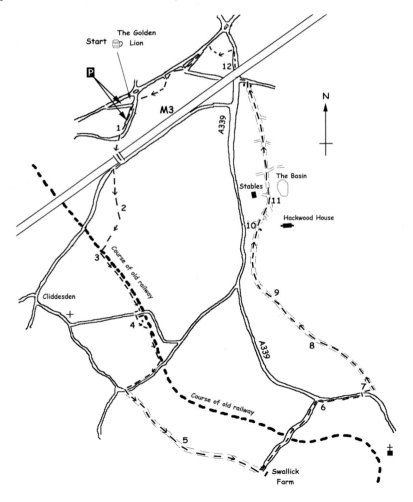

1. From the front of the pub, turn right and proceed down the old road, continuing straight on along the cycle path at the end, then cutting straight over the small bank and across Jays Close and straight on along the footpath opposite. This follows the original route of the Cliddesden Road before the arrival of the M3 and now leads you up and over a footbridge to rejoin its original route on the other side. Once you have descended back to road level, continue along the right hand side of the road until just past the end of the building opposite you see a footpath sign tucked into the hedge. Cross here and follow the sign into the hedge to pass through a squeezer stile.

2. The footpath cuts diagonally across a small field to the top corner where we pass through another squeezer, then through a small copse, and through another squeezer on the far side. This brings us to some fields where we proceed straight on just to the left of the hedgerow that confronts you at this point.

3. As we approach the corner of the field, a gap reveals itself in the corner. We pass through this gap crossing as we do the former trackbed of the Basingstoke and Alton Light Railway. Emerging into another field on the other side, turn left sticking to the hedgerow. Along here its possible to spot several of the metal fence posts that were the original boundary of the line before the hedgerow grew up to take over. Breathtakingly beautiful black and vermilion Cinnabar moths were the perfect compliment to the scanty array of Poppies lining the margin of this field as I walked this route in early summer.

4. When you reach the road, turn right past the front of the Railway Cottages, and then pick up the path that passes alongside them on the left. Shortly we pass what was the Station Masters house with in its garden a small square shed, all that remains of the Cliddesden railway station platforms and buildings. This was the station immortalised as Buggleskelly in the classic 1937 Will Hay film 'Oh! Mr Porter'. The line had closed a year earlier following a very chequered history, which included being lifted and sent in its entirety to the western front in WW1 and Cliddesden Station has probably seen more Will Hay fans since its closure than it ever saw passengers while it was open. The platform buildings themselves were little more than tin shacks but surprisingly one solitary example did manage to survive further down

the line where it nominally served the villages of Bentworth and Lasham until its was unceremoniously demolished in 2003. Once you've contemplating the archaeological significance of the lumps and bumps of the station field, continue along the field edge till you reach the lane. Don't drop down onto the road here, instead turn right along the top of the bank till you reach the footpath sign where we cross over and follow the byway opposite.

5. Though quite a steep climb, this track rewards you with a fine view across Basingstoke and down onto the stately lines of Hackwood House. Maps show our route over this hill once led from Cliddesden all the way to the now rather forlorn and isolated Winslade Church, but the path is now curtailed at Swallick Farm where we turn left along the tarmac road passing between redundant railway bridge abutments.

6. At the junction with the A339, turn right and stay on the verge, jumping carefully over the conveniently placed drainage ditches placed with due import for us pedestrians. Cars pass at great speed along here and I suggest you proceed to a point between the 'Reduce Speed Now' signs where there is a verge opposite that you can cross to, then cross over with great care.

7. Now on the opposite side of the A339, continue into the lay-by on the corner formed where the road was straightened in the 1950's. In the corner of the lay-by on the left we pass through a wooden kissing gate, which marks what was once a formal entrance into Hackwood Park complete with a gatehouse though this was demolished many years ago. Follow the green track signposted 'Footpath to Basingstoke' curving away slightly to the left.

8. Along the track we pass beautiful mature Elm and Beech trees as Hackwood House comes into view on the right. At the end we come to a metal kissing gate fitted with a cunning deer-proof bolt (deer not being ambidextrous of course).

9. Continuing straight on, we pass alongside a haha, which denotes the boundary of the more formal part of the grounds and onto what is now a gravel track. Ignore the track off to the left to pass alongside a row of young maple trees on the right and then more mature Sweet Chestnuts on the left.

10. Passing by a newly restored lodge, we come onto a tarmac road where we continue straight ahead over a cattle grid and past a large bollard fitted atop with an important

ancient and inscrutable metal device, probably used for parking horses.

11. Passing between the magnificent stable block with its little turret on the right and The Basin with its fountain on the left, continue straight on till you pass through the gates out of Hackwood Park and back onto a public road.

12. Cross over and turn left for a short walk to the A339. Turn right here, walk down to a point near the motorway bridge and again cross with great care. Continue along the A339 then turn left up a small incline, which takes you into Poynings Close. Cross over and turn down the small footpath just after No 12, which will take you to Grove Road just beside the garage. Turn left and turn up Skippetts Lane East, continuing straight at the end along the path by the fallen tree. This brings you back once again to Grove Road, but a few yards further along you can turn down the drive of ICS Solutions and turn up Skippetts Lane West just before you reach the barrier. Continue straight up Skippetts Lane West then along the short path with brings you out directly in front of the Golden Lion.

The Six Bells, Bramley

Having sheltered under the name of the Bramley Inn for several years, the current owners of the former Six Bells Hotel in Bramley decided that they preferred the original title and at the time of my visit were awaiting delivery of a new sign to complete its recent transformation, which includes a refurbished restaurant and bar and a new function and conference room. There is a very large garden, and the Sunday Roast on offer for £5.95 at the time of my visit could be washed down with a pint of the Hampshire Brewery's Ironside Best or Charles Wells' Bombadier.
Telephone 01256 881580

The pub is situated in The Street Bramley, just west of the level crossing.

Approx. distance of walk: 4 miles. Start at OS Map Ref SU 652595.

Parking is available in the car park of the village recreation ground off Minchens Lane opposite Stocks Farm.

An easy, flat walk with just three well-spaced stiles to negotiate, passing through woodland and along farm tracks to Bramley's splendid church.

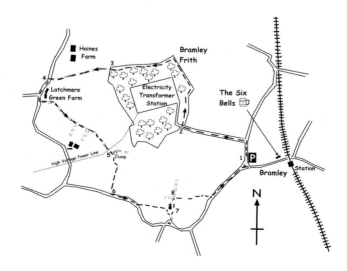

17

Walk No. 3

1. From the car park, exit onto Minchens Lane. Down the lane to the left is the old granary, balanced precariously on those familiar mushroom-like staddle stones, which used to keep the rats out but are now a more familiar sight as very valuable garden ornaments. We turn right, shortly passing the doctors surgery. Turn left when you reach a tarmac road with a signpost indicating bridleway leading to the Bramley Frith Education Centre.

2. Just before the second set of gates, we turn right to leave the tarmac road continuing along the bridleway. This lightly gravelled path is very easy to follow through the Frith as it skirts the powerful electricity transformer station now stationed at the heart of the wood. The ever-present hum of raw power a notable accompaniment along this first part of the walk. The use of the name Frith for this little wood probably indicates that it was here before the Norman Conquest. The electricity station is a more recent invader.

3. The hum fades as we move further north in the wood eventually reaching a junction in its northwest corner just after the path has turned sharp right. Ignore the path over two wooden sleepers straight on, instead going left over the more substantial bridge across a prominent water-filled ditch and over a stile. Follow the wide track straight ahead curving away to the left.

4. At the end of the track we cross over a stile alongside Latchmere Green Farm onto a little country road called Ash Lane. Turn left down the lane, shortly passing a joyful little Edward VII post box just after leaping past the junction with Frog Lane. A few metres further on, take the gravel track off to the left signposted footpath, following it round to the right after a short straight section.

5. Ignore the tracks off to the right towards the farm buildings until just after passing beneath some high power lines we reach a triangular section of gravel where the main track bears left. We go straight on onto a small flat grassy area to the right of a clump of bushes, turning left then right past a very large wooden fencepost following a narrow path with a hedgerow to our left.

6. We emerge onto the main Bramley Road alongside a heavily fortified pumping station. Cross over and turn left to proceed along the road. Ignore the first footpath sign you'll see shortly on the left to take the second which runs along to the right of the hedge you see in front of you (not along the gravel drive to the old school). You can forgo passing through the overgrown kissing gate in the middle unless you're particularly masochistic, keeping straight on alongside the hedge past the allotments towards the church.

7. A circuit around the outside of the church reveals many fine monuments though few perhaps as touching as the crude wooden cross apparently sculpted from redundant cot posts. At the other extreme, the naïve weather vanes depict the severed head of a Moroccan king, the rather grim family crest of the Brocas family who owned much of the land hereabouts until the end of the 19th century. The church is generally left open and I heartily recommend investing in both its guidebook and a copy of its churchyard trail to fully appreciate the abundant wealth of treasures that this marvellous church contains.

8. We exit the churchyard to the north through a little metal gate, past the Cross House church rooms. We pass to the right of the rather pretty Victorian schoolhouse, which closed to pupils in the 1950's and was replaced by a more modern building east of the railway line. Cross the stile and continue straight on up the dirt track turning sharp right immediately after the hedgerow alongside a footpath marker post. Follow the path along to a gap on the corner where we exit down a gravel drive to the right of a white garage. Turn right along the road till you reach the pub.

The Chineham Arms, Chineham

The Chineham Arms, like much of Chineham itself is a youthful freshfaced youngster particularly in the world of alehouses being built a mere 14 years ago in 1989. Despite its youth, the blue Cask Marque by the door shows that they know how to pull a pint here and though the range in this 'Fullers English Inn' is limited to London Pride, E.S.B and a single guest ale – Worthington 1744 whilst I was there - the quality of your pint is sure to be second to none. Currently managed by Ray Turnbill and his team, The Chineham Arms has one large bar and a separate restaurant area along with a large garden with benches outside. The recently revised menu features a much wider variety of dishes than in the past and though lacking the individual touch you might find at an independent pub, does offer an interesting range to choose from including several home-made dishes, and of course there are the usual range of sandwiches and jackets and slightly more exotic Nachos if your sombrero is that way inclined. Dogs are welcome on a lead and children before 18:00.

The pub is open 11-23:00 Monday to Saturday and 12-22:30 Sunday with food available 12-21:30 Monday to Saturday and 12-21:00 Sunday.

Telephone 01256 356404

Walk No. 4

Approx. distance of walk: 3 miles. Start at OS Map Ref SU 659557.

Parking is available alongside the pub on Hanmore Road. Please do not park in Renown Way.

The Manor of Chineham can be traced back to the Doomsday book and beyond but visitors searching for the village of Chineham even as recently as Edwardian times would have found little save for Chineham farm in what is now Popley, and a brick kiln and perhaps a few traces of deserted medieval village in what is now Daneshill. It was only during the post-WWII era that a string of houses and a couple of shops slowly appeared along the A33 between the railway bridge and the old Tollhouse to form anything approaching a small hamlet. There has been a smidgeon of development since then of course, and Chineham is now slightly bigger, but this much-liked suburb of Basingstoke hasn't entirely escaped its green and pleasant past and much countryside is still just an easy stroll away.

Though this walk can be muddy in places, its generally very easy going with only minor hills.

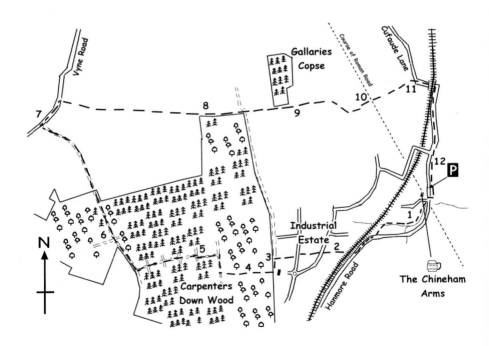

1. From the pub, cross Renown Way and you'll see our footpath on the right which runs alongside the culverted Petty's Brook, one of the tributaries of the River Loddon. Carry straight on past a small bridge along the tarmac path keeping the brook on your left, shortly crossing a wooden bridge then turning left to return to Hanmore Road alongside the Scout HQ. Continue along the right hand side of Hanmore Road past the bus stop and then we turn right by the metal fence through a tunnel and under the railway embankment.

2. Follow the path on the other side around to a road, cross over and carry straight on along the gravel path on the other side, shortly crossing a second minor road in the business park and continuing straight on between industrial buildings.

3. At the back of these buildings you'll come to a T-junction, here turn left past a sign saying 'no motor vehicles beyond this point'. Shortly, as we pass a red brick building on our left, turn down a narrow path off into the woods on the right passing an old abandoned well within a few yards.

4. As we move further into the wood, the path twists and turns around various obstructions but generally follows a straight line, after a while passing straight over a raised boundary with a ditch on the other side. Continue along the well-trodden path straight on till you come to a second boundary with an HCC marker post, cross the ditch after this post and turn right, shortly passing over a fallen pine tree. After crossing another ditch, we come to a fork in the path where we turn left along a gravelled path.

5. We come to another junction in the path shortly afterwards where we turn right onto a muddy track which then bears round to the left. Continue straight on crossing several other tracks and paths till eventually having passed a redundant wooden gate we come to another T-junction where we turn right staying just inside the woods.

6. Follow this path carrying straight on across a gravel track where our path becomes a lot wider on the other side, shortly passing a large metal tank on the right. Pass around the gate near the houses at the end of this section and continue along the gravel track, which will bring you out onto Vyne Road.

7. Turn right along the road passing an old gatehouse to the Vyne on the left. Shortly you'll come to our next path marked with a footpath sign on the right. The path leads into a field and we follow this along the right hand side, passing straight over a track and continuing on as the towers of Basingstoke come into view on the right.

8. At the corner of the field we reach Collett's Copse. Crossover the stile here and continue straight on in the next field along the left side of the copse. At the corner of the field, go through the gap by the marker post and straight across the deeply rutted track.

9. We now pass to the right of Gallaries Copse and then alongside a wire fence. At the corner of this field we cut through the gap around the end of this wire fence and then continue straight on along the right side of the next field. Where the field turns right, head towards the gap in the hedge on the corner and across a wooden stile continuing along the right hand side of the next field and following it round to the left.

10. At the end of this field we pass through another gap in the hedge into a small dell. Here we pass a sloping gully in the hedge on our right that is a rare visible trace of the course of the roman road from Silchester to Chichester. A rickety wooden bridge and a stile now lead us into the next field where we continue along the right hand field edge.

11. Pass through the metal gate on the corner past what appears to be a small section of the Berlin Wall and turn right along the road. This road has been known as Cufaude Lane for centuries, after the Cufaude family who built a moated manor house during the mediaeval period just to the north of our walk. The railway authorities use a different more logical system and you'll notice they call it Gaffier Lane Bridge when you pass under it as you continue on your way back to Chineham.

12. As you approach the Chineham signs, you can cross to the left and follow the route of the old road on the left till you see the Chineham Arms through the hedge on your right.

The Deane Gate Inn, Deane

The road from Overton to Basingstoke is full of swoops and hollows and the toll-gate at Deane crossroads must have made a welcome break for the horses after the rollercoaster ride that goes before. It's said that from this point Jane Austen would catch the stage to Basingstoke, and I'm sure we can equally speculate that on a hot summers day she may well have knocked back a quick rum and coke at the Deane Gate Inn while she was waiting. Externally this Inn has a timeless appearance although it is much altered and extended since those coaching days not least because of a car that crashed through it's side several years ago! It's currently owned by the Innspired group and Melanie and Nigel Steer have been running things for them for the past year, building up its reputation as a warm and friendly local. There is only one main bar but it twists around the house in such a way that its easy to believe there are several more and there are lots of comfortable nooks and crannies to tuck yourself into. There is also a large garden outside for long hot sunny days. The food is good and hot and several dishes on the specials board particularly caught my eye; Tom Yum prawns with a sweet chilli dip, Oven baked Tuna Steak on a bed of mixed leaves with asparagus and cherry tomatoes sprinkled with raspberry vinaigrette or how about the Tex-Mex special with ribs, wings, onion rings, garlic bread, chilli beef and salsa sauce. As well as the specials there is a regular menu along with the usual range of sandwiches, baguettes and Jacket Potatoes to enjoy. For lovers of real ale you can choose between Old Speckled Hen, Banks Bitter, Marston's Pedigree or the old dependable Courage Best. Children are allowed in the pub for meals and dogs providing they are on a lead.

Opening hours are 11-15:00 and 17:23:00 Monday to Saturday 12-17:00 Sundays – the pub is closed Sunday evenings. Food is available 12-14:30 and 18-21:00 Monday to Saturday and 12-16:30 Sundays.

Telephone 01256 780226

Approx. distance of walk: 6 miles. Start at OS Map Ref SU 570510.

Parking is available in the village hall car park or recreation ground car park in Church Oakley or by prior arrangement in the overflow car park of the Deane Gate Inn just across the lane to Steventon (Map Ref SU 548499) in which case start the walk at point 6.

This walk has a great deal to delight, the lovely little cottages in Deane, the glorious neo-gothic All Saints Church and almost stately Deane House, the magnificent trees in Oakley Park and finally the wonderful view downhill at the end towards St Leonard's Church in Oakley.

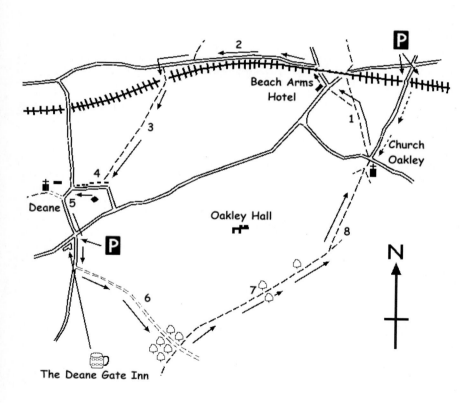

Walk No. 5

1. From the car park, we proceed along Station Road to the junction with Rectory Road opposite St Leonard's Church. On the corner to your right, you'll find a wooden kissing gate into the field. Pass through the gate and take a route diagonally across the field to the left, clipping the protruding corner of the hedgerow to the right to bring you to a stile. Cross the stile and continue along your diagonal route towards a gap in the far corner. Here we cross another stile then follow the path straight on keeping the hedge and fence to our left towards the Beach Arms.

2. At the end of this field, cross another wooden stile to bring us to the B3400 road. Cross the road carefully and follow the little road straight on between the Beach Arms and the bus garage. Pass under the railway bridge and then turn left down a country lane that was once a section of the old Harrow Way. Follow this road past Deane Down Farm, then just past the second house after the farm; take the footpath off to the left, where we join the route of the Wayfarers Walk long distance footpath.

3. Passing through a metal kissing gate, walk straight up the field and through another kissing gate hidden behind the tree at the top. We then cross a bridge over the railway line, which brings us into a large field. The path heads across this field diagonally to the right passing beneath the low voltage power cables ahead at a point midway between the supporting poles. As we reach the brow of the hill, Oakley Hall Conference Centre comes into view down to our left. Our path continues its route diagonally across this field from the brow directly towards the supporting pole of another low voltage power cable in the bottom right hand corner.

4. At this corner we pass through a gap to the left into another field where we continue our diagonal route across the field towards a group of houses on the far side where we reach the village of Deane. Pass through the gap in the hedge by the houses then follow the path to the right of farm buildings to the corner of a small green. Here turn left down a gravel track that brings us to a tarmac road. Turn right along the road and then left at the next junction

5. Passing the impressive Manor Farm building across the field to the left, continue along the road until you reach the footpath to All Saints Church on your right. This is a magnificent building, almost unchanged since it was built in 1818. On the ground, two unblemished and beautifully carved coade-stone pinnacles can be admired closely they have been waiting patiently for restoration to the tower for several years although there is nothing to indicate whether this will ever take place. At least here you can appreciate their finery in detail! Return to the road along the footpath and you can make a few admiring glances toward Deane House over to the left along the way where Jane Austen attended several dances. Though much enlarged, the central part of this side of the house is considerably older than the church and is believed to date from the 1680's. At the road turn right crossing the B3400 at the junction with care to reach the Deane Gate Inn.

6. From the pub, continue along the road until you reach a gravel track on the left in front of Cheesedown Cottages. Follow this track for about 1/2 mile along a tree lined section, then a clearer section where fields are in view on both sides till you approach a part where there is a small dense wood to the right of the track. We pass this with a line of oaks on our left to a crossroads with another track. Here we turn left along a wide grassy track and we get a good view over to the north on our left.

7. Follow along this dirt track to a point where it turns sharp right and where we continue straight on past a redundant stile into the former grounds of Oakley Park passing between a beautiful pair of elderly beech trees as we do so. A little further on, a rustic bench of old logs sits beneath another beautiful tree although this ones branches were too high for an amateur arborealist like myself to make a positive identification. Shortly we approach a line of trees crossing our path through which the Church of St Leonard's comes into view on our left. Pass through the gap in the hedge passing a fine old iron fence post in the middle and cross the pasture ahead diagonally to the right towards the fingerpost.

8. From the fingerpost take the left fork down the hill towards the church passing through three metal kissing gates and over a stile along the way. A path then leads you through the churchyard back to the road at the front of the church.

The Queens Inn, Dummer

A popular spot for local businessmen wishing to entertain their clients to lunch, The Queens Inn offers a vast and colourful menu and deservedly has recently been named as one of the top five food pubs in the Unique Pub Awards. Landlord Matthew Sadler is justifiably proud of its status and has striven hard to build its reputation.

The pub dates back as far as the 14th Century and there are comfortable, cosy nooks in the one main bar where you can tuck yourself away as well as the larger dining areas and small beer garden at the back. There is a large log fire in the winter.

I enjoyed a pint of Old Speckled Hen, and London Pride was also on offer along with the regular Courage Best.

The pub is open 11:30-15 and 18-23:00 Monday to Saturday and 12-15:00 and 19-22:30 Sunday with food available from opening time till 14:30 and until 21:30 in the evenings.

Telephone 01256 397367

Walk No. 6

The pub is situated at the southern end of Down Street in the village.

Approx. distance of walk: 7½ miles. Start at OS Map Ref SU 588460.

There are several spots to park along the verge on Up Street or between the Queen Inn and the Church.

Dummer, on the hilly side of Basingstoke is said to take it's name from 'hill by the water' although which particular water is open to debate. It has, without doubt one of the most attractive churches to be found on any of the walks in this book and also a joyful old folk song celebrating local cottiers and incumbents of long-ago. Presumably a medieval one-way system gave rise to its two imaginatively named main roads of Up Street and Down Street. This walk provides an undulating but relatively easy-going walk mainly along farm tracks. Slightly further up Down Street (if you'll forgive the pun) from the pub is the old village well, rather unusually operated by human-powered tread-wheel and to think, people usually move to the country to escape the rat-race.

1. We start the walk at the church. Although locked at the time of my visit this has generally been open in the past, and the interior has a great deal of interest including the gallery upstairs. However limiting myself to what was available at the time of my visit, the lych gate with its massive timbers taken from an ancient barn at Dummer Grange is a fitting memorial to the fallen of the village and leads you up to the wonderful porch with its feather-like shingle tiles over the entrance and wonderfully decorative flourishes above the tiny windows on the north side. Continuing round to the north, a truly diminutive priests door may cause speculation about the height of the clergy in the 13th century when this feature was added but adds further charm to the picture. In the

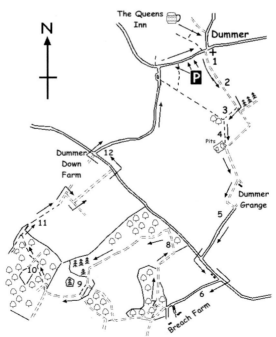

graveyard prominent cast-iron headstones pay tribute not only to the otherwise long-forgotten individuals who lie beneath, having weathered the test of time rather better than their stone contemporaries, but also to the foundry that made them which was just along the road in Up Street. We leave the churchyard by the lynch-gate and turn left along Up Street.

2. Passing Ivy Cottage with what appears to be Harry Potters Order of the Phoenix on it, we turn left along the bridleway signposted at the entrance to the Manor Farm housing development, continuing straight along the concrete track past the houses.

3. The track goes downhill, over a watercourse then back up the other side. Nearing the top, we approach a line of trees off to the left which once led up to Dummer's windmill, just before we reach these; our path is southwest, directly to the right. It runs through a gap in the fence across an open field towards the left tree of two large lone trees you can see directly opposite on the far side.

4. Having crossed the field you find yourself on a corner by a concrete water-trough. Here we turn left to follow a path diagonally across the field heading south. This brings us to another inside corner of the field and our path continues straight on into a small wood passing a large disused pit on the right.

5. We emerge onto a dirt track, which we now follow to the right continuing along it as it turns left and then heads downhill. We take the fork to the right near some cottages, and then turn left and downhill shortly to reach what is a tarmac drive but which could easily be a minor road. We turn right along this drive, which does bring us to a minor road where we turn left.

6. We follow this road past Burton and Ash Cottages on the right and then turn right along the signposted right-of-way towards Breach Farm. Keep straight on past the turnings for Breach Cottage and Breach House and onto a gravel track.

7. We pass a private track shortly on the right, and then just before our original track comes out of the woodland and onto open fields we turn right along a grassy track. I surprised a Hare as I reached the field here and after looking around briefly he shot off at a colossal pace. Follow this short little track and where we reach a much clearer track across our path, turn left along it.

8. We now follow this track for about a mile and a half. Until comparatively recently, it ran through Popham Down Wood, but now skirts the edge of what remains. Along this track I came across a beautiful stoat that had obviously died only very recently. Its sleek red-brown fur contrasting sharply with its creamy white belly and the distinctive black tip of its tail. I felt obliged to move his little body into the hedgerow before continuing.

9. After a long section uphill, the track turns left across a large grassy open area. Somewhat bizarrely this is called 'The Holt 'on recent maps. Holt being another name for a wood, it's perhaps not the most appropriate choice for the lack of one! We turn right to follow the finger post across the grassy area to a thin line of trees along the top. Here you'll find a marker post where we turn right along a nicely wooded path.

10. After a long relatively straight section, the path turns sharp left where it meets a track by another finger post. We however continue straight on along narrow path into the woods, shortly crossing a second track (with large wooden gates to the right) and then back deep into the wood. In a while we pass an old oil drum on our left before emerging into a small field. Turn right along the edge of the field then left at the corner to reach another track, which continues back into the woods to the right. We follow this for a few yards before our path cuts back into the woods on the left by a marker post.

11. The path through the woods is quite clear and easy to follow and we ignore a track that crosses our path, continuing straight on past a marker post and past another abandoned oil drum. Eventually you will reach a signpost in the wood with a bridleway indicated both left and right. We go right; shortly to pass another large abandoned pit on our right as our little wooded path leads us downhill.

12. At the bottom of the hill we reach a small wooden gate and we pass through this and turn right up a much wider track. At the top of the hill we find an identical gate on our left, which we pass through onto a grassy path beside but fenced off from a field. Follow this path straight down the hill where we exit through another gate and onto a minor road. Turn right along the road and then left at the junction opposite Dummer Down Farm. This road is known as Dummer Down Lane and leads us back to Up Street where we turn right to take us back to the church.

The Northbrook Arms, East Stratton

The village of East Stratton is where I think I found the answer to that age-old riddle, "Why did the chicken cross the road?" admittedly poultry are not renown for their pluck or intelligence, but the nonchalant air with which this particular fluffy, eagle-eyed bantam headed straight across the road for the pub surely answered this particular riddle once and for all whilst graphically demonstrating the splendid tranquillity of this lovely village.

Formerly known as The Plough, The Northbrook Arms is a fine rural, Victorian Freehouse, which Landlord David Sheaff took on just over six months prior to my visit. The Plough Bar is light, spacious and airy and there is also a cottage-like dining room a family room and a large garden at the front. Overall the atmosphere is sedate, calm and jovial and something of a contrast to David's very lively approach towards the range of food and ales on offer. Most pubs have a guest ale or two, which they change occasionally, The Northbrook Arms has hosted nearly fifty different ales in the last four months and there are apparently many more to come to keep the thirsty, inquisitive cliental happily quenched. I found Gales H.S.B, Gales Pompey Premier, Otter Bitter from the Otter Brewery in Devon and 'Our Ken', a medium dark ale with a smooth bitter finish and an ABV of 4.5 from the Cottage Brewing Company on tap, but you can be sure this line-up will have changed by the time you get there. The Ploughman's lunches are equally diverse with Double Gloucester and Herb, Wensleydale and Cranberry, Cornish Tiskey and Cornish Varg – wrapped in nettles - welcome alternatives to the more traditional cheeses. There is a list of delectable daily specials alongside such popular favourites as Banger and Mash or Homemade Steak and Ale Pie and there is a traditional roast on Sundays. Should the line-up of ales provoke you into staying rather longer than planned, you'll be pleased to know that Bed and Breakfast is also available at very reasonable rates!

The Northbrook Arms is open 11-23:00 Monday to Saturday and 12-22:30 Sunday. Food is available all the time!

Telephone 01962 774150

The Northbrook Arms is in the middle of East Stratton

Approx. distance of walk: 4 miles. Start at OS Map Ref SU 543398.

The landlord of the Northbrook Arms was more than happy for walkers to park in the car park at the rear of the pub at the time of my visit but as always it is a good idea to ask permission at the time of your walk particularly for a large party. Otherwise there is room for cars to be parked in the road outside.

George Dance the Younger made his name as the architect of Newgate Prison. Happily he relaxed his style somewhat when commissioned in 1803 by Sir Francis Baring, multi-millionaire founder of the Baring Brothers Banking firm and owner of nearby Stratton Park to build five estate houses in East Stratton to replace those Baring had flattened to expand the parks formal gardens. Such philanthropy was repeated by a later Baring who was equally happy to build a shiny new church so that he could demolish the tatty, original one on his doorstep. Today the once-huge Stratton Park estate is a shadow of its former self, the formal gardens and planted groves almost indistinguishable from the surrounding countryside and the heart of the estate pierced by the M3. Ironically after all that work by the Barings, it's now the villagers of East Stratton who find themselves in picturesque isolation.

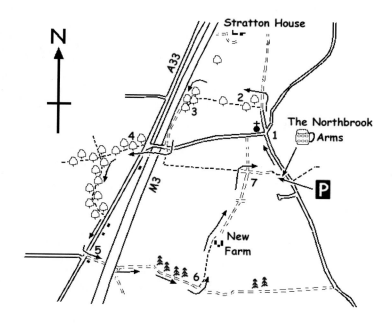

Walk No. 7

1. Starting from the pub, turn left and head north along the main street. At the junction to the right of the church, cross over and continue straight on to the left of the war memorial down the road marked 'No Through Road' shortly passing on the right what must be the most rural post office anywhere in Hampshire. Until the expansion of Stratton Park, this would have been the main road and we would still be heading into the village rather than away from it.

2. In a short distance, just before you come into Stratton Park, look out for a path leading off to the left into the woodland. Follow this path through the trees and continue straight on over the stile at the end, then to the right of a row of trees. There was a notice here to 'Beware of the Bull' during my visit, but the bull was notable only by its absence. Up on the right you can see the 'new' Stratton Park house, built on the site of its Georgian namesake in 1963. The portico of the original manor house was left as an amusing little garden ornament.

3. Cross another wooden stile on the other side of the field and follow the path straight on into the woods looking out for a green FP arrow on a marker post not too far ahead where the path bears left. Though shrouded behind trees, the noise of the M3 becomes more notable here particularly once we pass the remains of the old walled gardens of Stratton Park House buried in the woods. Shortly we cross another stile, and then turn left down a track that runs parallel to the M3.

4. At the end of the track we meet the road back into East Stratton. Unless you want a particularly short walk, turn right here and cross the bridge over the M3. At the junction with the A33, cross straight over then turn left and then shortly right to follow the bridleway signposted just behind the road signs. This runs along a narrow coppice known as Chapel Avenue as it links the two churches of Micheldever and East Stratton.

5. Shortly, where you come to an obvious crossroads with another path, turn left to follow another path still within the woods. Follow this path bearing left after a while until you eventually rejoin the A33. Cross over, back to the footpath on the other side and then turn right alongside the A33 for a short distance, turning left along the bridleway you'll reach just before the turning on the right towards Micheldever and Stoke Charity.

6. After passing under the M3 don't follow the more obvious track to the right but carry straight on instead past a metal gate and along a green track which runs down the left hand side of the field. Follow this track until you reach another track off to the left where we head towards some farm buildings you can see on the top of the hill. This farm is known as New Farm, but clearly its not all that new.

7. Follow the track keeping to the hedge on the left and passing to the left of the farm buildings. On the other side we follow what is now a gravel track and continue straight up the hill. Continue straight on at a crossroads where other tracks lead into fields and then turn right at the next crossroads alongside a telegraph pole and this follow this path back into the pub car park.

The Royal Oak, Ecchinswell

I admit I failed to notice if there was still a large Oak tree amongst all the other trees around the garden of the Royal Oak, distracted by the far more conspicuous wooden ducking stool - a popular nautical activity throughout the pubs May Fair - and equally conspicuous, the enormous thatched hut that is Ed's Rum Shack, a joyful memorial to a late but very notable regular. Serving the aforementioned tipple on Friday nights and Sunday evenings during the summer months and featuring what I can only describe as Flintstone-style chunky furniture, each piece hewn with a chainsaw from a solid log taken from the trunk of what must have started out as a very large tree!

Ann Noonah has run this popular 14th century village pub for the last seven years, building up its enviable reputation as a happy, much-liked watering hole that seems equally popular with young and old. Whether this is down to the pubs spacious, comfortable bars or to Ann's very extensive Curry menu I don't know, but alongside the usual snacks, sandwiches and baguettes, there is a wide selection of freshly prepared delights to tempt the taste buds, you might like to try the Chicken Balti or perhaps the tuck in to a Murgh Tikka Matarb.

Always on tap are Flowers Original, Spitfire and Greene King IPA with the occasional guest ale alongside.

The pub is open 12-23:00 Monday to Saturday and 12-22:30 Sunday with food available 12-14:00 and 1830-21:15 Monday to Friday and all day weekends.

Telephone 01635 298280

Walk No. 8

The pub is situated on the main road through the village.

Approx. distance of walk: 6 miles. Start at OS Map Ref SU 500597

Parking is available in the lay-by opposite the school or in the large car park outside the village hall and playground.

In far-off less hygienic days, Ecchinswell went under the rather unfortunate name of Itchingswell, not that its residents were any more unsanitary than the rest of the population you understand, in truth the names origins are so obscure that nobody really knows, they don't appear to be derived from the River Itchen which is miles away, the river flowing through the village being a tributary of the River Enborne. If you want to find out for certain I suppose you'll have to start from scratch. There is quite a hilly start to this walk, but you are richly rewarded when you reach the top!

1. From the car park opposite the school, turn right along the main road. I particularly enjoyed the old school building and schoolmasters house along here with their indulgent confectionary of Victorian embellishment and something akin to a gothic rocketship perched on top of the old schoolhouse. Turn left just before the pub along the road, which is signposted 'Kingsclere 3'. We pass over and then alongside the little rivulet, which flows behind the pub and its ducking stool, and then turn right where the road turns left across a little footbridge and onto a grassy path.

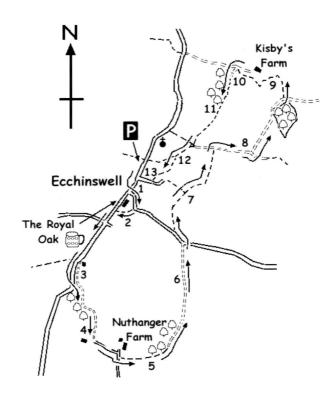

2. Very quickly we come to a clearing, empty now but once the site of the village church. Its location right next to the river was far from ideal and it was demolished in 1884 following years of dank decline, replaced by a new church built on higher ground further up the road. Tucked away over in the weeds to the left is the stone slab that marks the grave of Churchwarden John Digweed who was the only person known to be buried within its grounds. Continue along the path and turn left at the road past the lovely old vicarage.

3. We pass a small-detached cemetery on the left and then an ornithological menagerie at the small cottage opposite the drive to Sydmonton Court. Just past the cottage we take the grassy track on the left that gradually veers away from the road. Where the path meets a field alongside a metal gate, don't enter the field but take the path beside it alongside the woodland on the right.

4. We now enjoy quite a steep climb but are richly rewarded along the way by some wonderful views back down across the village. Nearing the top we pass through two small green metal gates onto a tarmac road near some farm buildings. Keep going on up the road and turn left at the top away from the farmhouse.

5. Staying on the tarmac, go right of the stable block then turn right after passing through a white metal gate. A few yards on turn left along a signposted footpath, following the left hand edge of the field. Across to your right, the grassy hill is known as Watership Down, apparently quite well known for some book or something.

6. Just before our path turns left at the end of a long hedge, it's worth a short diversion straight on to get a good view down the valley over to the left known as Hollywell Bottom. Returning to the left hand edge of the field, begin the descent down the vale passing to the right of a row of oak trees. Shortly we turn left into the wood then right, down a narrow track with trees on either side. Follow this all the way to a small road.

7. Turn left along the road for a little way to a stile on the right. Cross the stile then head diagonally across the field to the left towards a gate in the bottom left corner. Cross the stile here and across a little wooden bridge to follow the path along the left hand edge of the field. A gap in the hedge is a shortcut back to the village if you wish, but we carry on past this, rounding a curve to the left to a

corner where the field turns sharp right. We continue straight on over some wooden planks through a gap in the hedge and straight across the next field towards a gap on the far side.

8. Through the gap we come to a tee junction with another path where we go right, continuing straight on along the right and hedgerow where we enter a field and then right onto a separate path again by a post with a blue arrow. Shortly we reach a gravel track across our path where we turn left.

9. Follow the track as it curves around a wood on the right and then just as we pass a hedgerow on the left, turn left by a marker post along the edge of the field. Shortly we pass through a gap in the hedge marked by another post turning right in the next field along the right hand hedgerow. Keep following the hedge left then right then left again until you see a gap leading to a stile just past Kisby's Farm.

10. Cross the stile, then a little wooden bridge over a stream, then a 2nd stile into a field. The path here meanders in a roughly straight line over to a gate you can see up ahead just to the right, as you get nearer to the gate you'll see a stile in the corner which is where you leave this field.

11. Over the stile climb down to the track turning left and then immediately left again along a footpath signposted through the wood. Follow this path along crossing out of the wood over a stile alongside a metal gate then continuing in the same direction across a grassy field along the right hand hedgerow.

12. We leave this field by another stile in the bottom corner alongside a wooden gate. Follow the path to the left through a small copse and then turn left at the track by the gate turn right in front of the brick pumping house and follow a muddy path through a narrow thicket turning left where you reach two small wooden footbridges, over the bridges and then over a stile. Ignore the arrow on the stile and turn right along the right hand edge of the field which will bring you to another stile just to the right of the white house.

13. Follow the narrow path alongside the fence and turn right where you reach a tarmac road. Past a spectacular old barn and the wonderful old mill house to return to the main road. Turn left and make your way to the Royal Oak for a well-earned pint.

The George & Dragon, Swallowfield

The pub is situated along the main road between Swallowfield and Farley Hill.

Though Landlady Karine Spain happened to be out at the time of my visit, several of her most attractive team were on hand at the time to help advise and assist. 'People come from miles around for our shoulders' the young lady remarked. I smiled politely then blushed as the others made clear that the shoulders in question were half shoulders of lamb prepared – along with other epicurean delights - to such perfection by Chef Gerry Coetzee that the George and Dragon was voted 2003's Berkshire Pub-restaurant of the year. The team promise Real Ales, Real Wine and Serious Food and further comment seems superfluous other than to say that this smashing little freehouse dates back to the 15th-century when it started life as a small farm.

The pub is open 12-23:00 Monday to Saturday and to 22:30 Sunday with food available 12-14:30 and 19-21:30. Dogs and children are welcome in the areas away from the bar.

Telephone 01189 884432

Approx. distance of walk: 4½ miles. Start at OS Map Ref SU 758643.

There is space for several cars along the main street in Farley Hill Village near to the school.

Farley Hill lies within the parish of Swallowfield just on the Berkshire side of the Hants/Berks border. Whilst altitudinanlly, architecturally and historically this small hill is of minimal significance, Farley Hill is nevertheless remarkable for having been located in the county of Wiltshire until 1844.

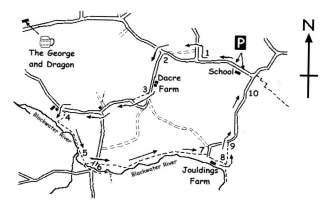

1. We begin outside Farley Hill School and proceed west along the footpath on the same side of the road. Cross over at the junction with Castle Road and walk up Castle Road past the elaborate gateposts that mark the entrance to the King George V playing field. A short distance further on, take the byway signposted on your left which runs behind the playing field.

2. Where this path rejoins the road, continue along the right hand side for about 100 yards to a place where you can see it's clear to cross, then continue on and turn down Sandpit Lane

3. Quarter of a mile down the lane, we turn up the signposted track going up into a field on our right. At the top of a small bank, follow the marker post to the left, then follow the right hand side of the field to the top corner by a very dilapidated shed where the path continues through the hedge and down some steps back to the lane.

4. Turn right along the lane, keeping right at the junction by Sandpit Farm, after about quarter of a mile we come to a public footpath sign on the left where we turn and cross a little bridge and then a stile.

5. At the end of this path we reach another stile, cross this and turn left following the well-worn path through the grassy field alongside The Broadwater. Shortly we pass the point where the Blackwater and Whitewater Rivers meet and after this head towards the metal bridge you can see up ahead.

6. We don't actually cross this bridge; instead we turn left and follow the path to a metal gate. Passing through the gate (or over the stile if you're that way inclined) we cross over Ford Lane passing a very deep ford on our right which makes this point a remarkable popular location for 3-point turns. It also marks the point at which the roman road known as 'The Devil's Highway' crossed the river and where if you crossed the ford you would leave Berkshire and enter Hampshire. We remain in Berkshire however and follow the public footpath sign on the other side of the lane into the next field.

7. We now follow this path through several fields and although it isn't always in view, the Blackwater River is never more than a few yards away. Towards the end of this section where there is an open view of the river the path became indistinct due to earthworks. However if you continue towards the end of the field a stile will eventually come into view over to the left and we head for the stile.

8. Crossing the stile leads us to Jouldings Lane. Here turn right and then almost immediately left to take the footpath signposted on the opposite side over another stile and past the front of Jouldings Farm. The path follows the edge of the field for a short distance then crossing another stile, we pass along a narrow section between hedges.

9. At the end another stile brings us to an open field where we turn left keeping to the left hand hedgerow. Shortly we reach a small fish pond, which we pass to the left over two more stiles then crossing the last part of the field and another stile to return us to Jouldings Lane.

10. Turn right along Jouldings Lane, up the hill past Cheriton, Hill and Hollycrest Farms to return to the main road through Farley Hill, where we turn left to return to the school.

The Lion & Lamb Bistro, Farnham

Hiding behind what was once the Lion and Lamb Hotel, in a space that was almost cleared and filled with warehouses in the 1920's lies the venerable Lion and Lamb Yard. In days of old the stabling and storage area for the Hotel, it was extended in the 1980's and now provides another interesting and rewarding avenue for Farnham's many visitors to explore. One of its star attractions is the Lion and Lamb Bistro, a warm and welcoming establishment in the old part of the yard which first became a tea room just after the war but which has only really blossomed since it was taken on by the resourceful paring of Ondie Macleod and Anne McCulloch some four years ago. Without abandoning its traditional tearoom origins, they have developed a much wider and more sophisticated menu of home cooked dishes using freshly prepared and carefully selected ingredients.

Whether you opt for a traditional Cream Tea, a Ciabatta, Pannini or sandwich stuffed with one of the vast assortment of delicious fillings or something more substantial such as their delicious Beef and Guinness pie – tender pieces of steak cooked gently with a Guinness gravy and served with seasonal vegetables and potatoes or Salmon and Herb Tagliatelle – Pan fried fillet of Salmon on top of herb pasta with a walnut and horseradish cream, your first visit to the Lion and Lamb Bistro is unlikely to be your last.

The Bistro is open from 08:30 to 17:00 Monday to Saturday.

Telephone 01252 715156

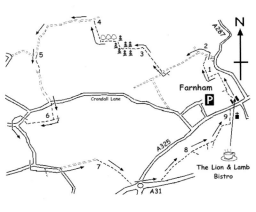

Approx. distance of walk: 6 miles. Start at OS Map Ref SU 838468.

Parking is available in the pay and display car park to the rear of the Lion & Lamb Yard.

Farnham offers so many delights, it would be easy to fill whole books with its virtues and as several people already have I shall keep this brief! This walk takes in just a tiny portion of the many fine attributes of this town with some great views, some interesting scenery culminating with the stark contrast between the open flood plains of the River Wey and this historic town and its church.

1. From the car park we head north along a narrow grassy path you'll find signposted near the top right corner. It's straight but quite steep. Towards the top we turn left onto another path, which takes us flat across the slope alongside a wire mesh fence. Turn right at the marker post at the end, up some steps and straight on across the field at the top to the hedge on the far side.

2. At the hedge turn round for a fine view across the town, then continue on through the gap ahead, straight over a short stretch of field to turn right at a marker post on the corner along a narrow path between wooden fences. At the end turn left along the road past the beautiful gates on the left into Castle Field. Shortly after we turn left along the footpath signposted along a gravel track next to Falcon House.

3. Keep straight on to the point where the main path jinks sharp left where we take an enclosed path off to the right passing a derelict and redundant stile. We proceed up the hill with a large bomb-hole beyond the trees off to the right. At the top we cross over a stile and turn left across the enclosure to exit by another. This takes us down through a lovely woodland glade and over a tiny brick bridge. We follow the path right on the other side where steps take us up and out via another stile.

4. Follow the path up the right hand edge of this field past three lone oaks and then sharp right through black metal gates straight across the field ahead to a kissing gate on the far side, across a small enclosure and through another kissing gate onto a tarmac road.

5. We proceed to the right along this road where I arrived just in time for a huge Heron to take off from the small pond on the right. Just round the corner on the right Ewshot Hall stands prominent in the distance just over the border in Hampshire. Stay on this road curving left at a white gate then round and downhill. After a small bridge the road turns sharp right while we carry straight on along the footpath ahead through a small wooden gate. Continue straight on through the next wooden gate and along a gravel drive to a road.

6. Cross over and up the bank to the left to a stile, then straight up the field towards a fingerpost on the crest where there are good views all round. From the post turn right along the brow of the field following the marker post shortly to pass along the fence to the right of the farm exiting the field by a gate. Turn onto the road to the right and then left along it. Turn right at the junction and down the Dippenhall dip past the old quarry workings on the right.

7. Turn left at the junction past the Old Barn along Runwick Lane continuing straight on shortly along a concrete track towards Potts Farm. We go straight on past the farm buildings on either side onto a mud track turning right where we come to a metal gate alongside a copse and continuing on along the left hand hedgerow of this field, exiting by a stile in the corner onto a narrow grassy path between hedgerows. At the end turn left over an abandoned section of the A31 alongside Cox Bridge and up the bank to the roundabout.

8. Turn left to cross over the road into Farnham then follow the verge alongside the A31 dual-carriageway to a 'Parking 250 yards' sign where you will find a stile down the bank to your left. Turn right over the stile and our path lies diagonally across this field to the right heading through the gap where the field narrows between hedges. Cross a stile at the end and like me you might wonder when the metal gate alongside was last opened. We now follow a well trodden path in the next meadow to the right of the cemetery continuing straight on past rusty old metal fence posts behind a large brick building. Where other paths go left and right here we continue straight on through a hedge into another field, past a house and straight across a gravel footpath, then over a footbridge onto a tarmac path turning left where the church comes into view

9. Follow the path along and into St Andrews churchyard. Turning left to exit by a narrow cobbled path, which brings us out on West Street, the Lion and Lamb Bistro is a few yards down the road to the right in Lion and Lamb Yard.

The Vine, Hannington

Few pubs can boast their own website, but if you're the type of person who enjoys a dabble on the net then visit www.hanningtonvine.com for all the latest information on Hannington's 17th century Inn. Technology aside, this pub is proud to offer all those good old-fashioned qualities of fine beer, excellent food and great service but you'll have to visit the pub to try these as virtual reality is no substitute for such virtues in reality. Martyn Osment and Anita Baker are the hosts of this large comfortable pub, which features one large bar with a conservatory and a separate restaurant area and also a large garden to the rear with a children's play area. The pub has always been popular with walkers and cyclists in the area and was originally called The Wellington Arms back in the 1950's when the good Duke owned most of the lands hereabouts. Today many come from far afield just for the food which includes such delights as 'Old Smokey' – Flaked, smoked haddock in a cream tomato, white wine and cracked pepper sauce topped with grated cheddar cheese or Stilton Chicken – Tender breast wrapped in smoked bacon and covered in a rich Stilton sauce amongst many others on the extensive menu.

The Vine is open 11-15:00 and 18-23:00 Tuesday to Saturday (closed Monday) and 12-16:00 Sundays with food available 11-14:00 and 18-22:00 Tuesday to Saturday and 12-15:00 Sundays.

Telephone 01635 298525

Approx. distance of walk: 8 miles. Start at OS Map Ref SU 538554

There is ample parking at the Vine and around the village green.

At 550ft above sea level, Hannington is one of the highest villages in Hampshire and the nearby Transmitter relay station at Cottington's Hill can be seen from almost every walk in this book. The location makes much of this walk exposed, often windy and with some steep climbs, perhaps the most strenuous of all the walks in this book. However on a clear day its route along the ridge of the North Downs offers spectacular views and if you take up this challenge, ensures you'll be richly rewarded for your endeavours.

1. We start at Hannington's large, picturesque and seemingly ancient village green, which in fact only dates back as far as the 1960's. Prior to that, two large and rather unsavoury ponds occupied this site known locally as 'the docks'. One pond had steep sides and was fenced around, and originally provided the village with its water supply, the other was a shallow affair, set out to quench the thirst of passing cattle providing they kept clear of the deep sticky mud that surrounded it which was said to have swallowed whole several less-fortunate beasts. Make your way over to the Millennium Milestone on the greens eastern flank and after you've admired the engraved stonework on top showing nearby landmarks, take the road directly opposite signposted to Ibworth.

2. After a short way, take the track on your left signposted footpath, directly opposite the quaint thatched cottage. Passing the village playground over the hedge on your right you'll soon reach an open field where

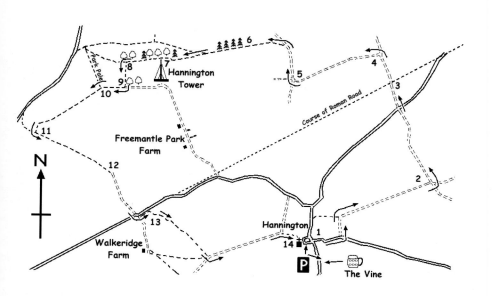

we bear right along a gravelled bridleway. There is a signpost for this in the hedge on the left, but you needed a machete to see it at the time of my visit. As we amble towards what looks like a prehistoric burial mound but is actually a modern concrete reservoir, the view south (on your right) is quite good providing a little taster for what is to come. Continue on, till you reach the junction at the corner of the small wood where we now take the track to the left. Hannington's transmission tower is particularly prominent only a mile or so over to the northwest. Initially the tower only carried BBC2 transmissions and it was during this period in the early 70's that it was mysteriously taken over by 'aliens' for just one night, transmitting greetings from another planet to rather baffled television viewers throughout the surrounding area before being successfully retaken by unarmed technicians the following day.

3.Follow the track down the rolling hill, at the foot of which we cross a minor road. Just to the east along this road another crossroads marks a spot known as Sawyer's Grave, where four woodcutters are said to have fought each other to the death in the 18th century and been buried along with their saw's. We go straight across and up the steep climb on the other side to the top of Plantation Hill. Halfway up we cross the now invisible route of the Portway, a Roman road from Salisbury to Silchester which for all its straightness must have been almost as steep as the hill that you're now climbing.

4. As you crawl exhausted to the top and Plantation Farm begins to creep slowly into view ahead, pause for a breath and take in the view over to the east (on your right) before proceeding along the well-defined track on your left. Shortly we pass another concrete burial mound before some great views open out to the north.

5. Where the track curves right at the next hedgerow and we come to a sort of crossroads alongside a gigantic plastic water butt up in the trees, follow the track to the right up and over the crest – not directly towards Hannington Tower as this isn't a right of way. Once you are over the crest, there is a short steep descent with hedgerows on both sides. As you emerge from these, look out for the stile on your left, which is our next path.

6. Crossing the stile, we now follow the path climbing along the top of this field. Keeping the barbed wire fence to our left we shortly enter four rows of pine trees planted in hon-

our of the Queens Coronation. In the distance to the northwest you can see laid out before you some of the gallops and horseracing stables and for which Kingsclere has been famous since the 1700's. The more athletic among you might even be tempted to try out the series of horse jumps we meet as we progress along this path, but I suggest you save your energy as there is another steep climb ahead.

7. Reaching a metal gate at the end of this path, almost directly alongside Hannington Tower, cross the stile to it's right and follow the clearly defined path along the top edge of the woods that make up Freemantle Park Down.

8. Reaching another stile on your left along this path (where footpaths are signposted in either direction but not over the stile!) we cross the stile for a short, steep, exhilarating climb through the open field keeping the barbed wire fence to our left.

9. Pause for breath when you reach the small copse at the top, turn round and you can admire the magnificent view east and west and all the way north to the Chilterns. Here we sit alongside medieval terraces and banks, which mark the site of an ancient house. This house is said to have had a very large and very deep well and local legend has it that two ducks, put down the well in the course of some bizarre experiment emerged a considerable time later at Kingsclere Mill far off in the valley below. The unfortunate birds were completely unharmed save that both had lost all their feathers during the experience. Much of what you see before you was taken over by the military during WW2, and it took quite a battle by the council to save it from target practice and military exercises.

10. Having plucked up enough resolve to continue on your way up hill, you'll shortly come to an endearingly post-modern metal stile at the top. Here we turn right, directly across the open field making for the wooden stile you can see over on the far side. Our route here follows an old track known as King John's Road, which about 800 years ago led to a Royal lodge traditionally believed to have been sited at nearby Freemantle Park Farm. This lodge was in the heart of the extensive Freemantle Deer Park, one old boundary of which - a 'Park Pale' as its known – still exists as the raised earthwork over on your right just as you meet the stile.

11. Crossing over the double stile, follow the

rather feeble hedge along the left hand side of the next field, which eventually curves round to the left and brings you to another stile by a white gate. Here we join the Wayfarers Walk, a long distance footpath established in 1981 from Inkpen Beacon in the north on the Hampshire/Berkshire border all the way down to Emsworth on the south coast. You'll be pleased to know you haven't got quite that far left to go as you cross the stile and follow the path to your left keeping to the right hand side of the field.

12. As you reach the top corner of this field, the path falls between two hedges eventually opening out with a good view south over Overton Mill, Overton village and to the hills beyond North Waltham. Continue along the path downhill till you meet a minor road.

13. Turn left for about 50 yards, and then take the footpath signposted along the edge of the field by the bridleway to Walkeridge Farm, keeping the hedge on your left. Turn right after a short distance to follow the footpath marked by the yellow arrow to the left of the dilapidated farm building. The otherwise unremarkable field on your right was the scene of a forced landing for a light aircraft in 1996 making a rather ham-fisted

attempt to smuggle drugs into the country from Holland. Although the plane landed in one piece, the passenger alighting in rather a panic with a briefcase full of drugs in hand unfortunately failed to notice that the propeller at the front of the plane was still rotating. Apparently he survived, but you might want to watch where you tread. Where you meet the junction with other paths, go right.

14. This final stretch of path toward Manor Farm is all the more attractive for the substantial hedges on either side. Follow this path until you reach the wooden gate marked 'Footpath Only'. Follow the grassy path to the right of the big hedge and around the barn turning left along the gravel drive of Manor Farm to return to Hannington's Green. All Saint's Church warrants a visit before you make your way to the Vine for well-deserved refreshment. A blocked up 15th century doorway (only visible from outside) on the south wall stands next to an Anglo-Saxon sundial uncovered during repairs in 1970 and thought to have moved here from the original south wall when the church was enlarged around 1180. Points worthy of note inside are the two etched windows by Sir Laurence Whistler and the villages Millennium tapestry.

Miranda's Coffee Shop, Kingsclere

At one time the village betting office and more recently a picture framers, Miranda Walsh opened this very welcome little teashop in the heart of Kingsclere in December 2002. Despite its small size, it quickly attracted a large and loyal following for its delicious freshly made sandwiches, home made quiches and many other delights including slightly out-of-the-ordinary soups which change daily and are something of a speciality with fresh pea, mint and lemon accompanying rather more traditional lines at the time of my visit. Today's papers are always on hand and there is a children's corner full of distractions so you can sit back, relax and enjoy a slice of their scrumptious baked apple and blackberry pie served with custard, ice cream, cream or even all three!

Once you've had your fill, you'll find there are also a large range of preserved epicurean delicacies to tempt you such as Sun dried tomatoes in olive oil, Duck Pate with Armagnac and specially imported from Shropshire - Milly Hunters handmade cakes – 'take a taste and you won't be able to leave without one!'

Miranda's is open 08-18:30 Monday to Friday, 08-17:00 Saturday and 10-16:00 on Sundays.

Telephone 01635 299110

Approx. distance of walk: 5½ miles. Start at OS Map Ref SU 525588.

Parking is available in the Anchor Yard Car Park signposted off Swan Street and along nearby Larch Road and St Mary's Road.

With the thundering traffic along the A339 safely diverted to the North, Kingsclere has returned to pre-1970's levels of calm allowing years of traffic grime to be stripped back to reveal a joyous variety of old and illustrious buildings throughout its heart. Quite where the 'clere' part of Kingsclere originates from, historians are still divided on, but the King bit seems to have been added around the 13th century to denote the ownership of the lands hereabouts by the monarchs of the time even though it had been a royal manor for several hundred years before. Famously, local legend has it that the church weather vane resembles a bed bug, erected by order of King John after a very unsettled night as a guest of the town.

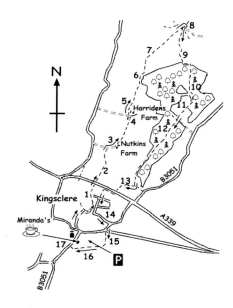

and then pass over a little metal footbridge and then a little wooden footbridge out onto another grassy meadow where we continue along the left hand side.

3. Shortly our path moves left around a line of White Willows alongside the stream before we reach a metal kissing gate at the top of this field. We cross the stream here over a quaintly angled wooden bridge and then follow a narrow grassy path pinned between a hedgerow and a fence. At the end we emerge onto a tarmac drive where we turn right towards Nutkin's Farm, passing through the gateposts over a concrete bridge and then turning left over some grass towards a stile.

4. Cross the stile and head diagonally over to the right to meet and proceed along the right side of the field. At the top of this field, cross the stile just to the right of the metal storage shed.

5. At the front of the shed, cross the gravel track and follow the direction of the footpath sign over to the middle of a grassy strip where you will find a stile carefully hidden in the ditch. Cross the stile and a small stream and then up the other side of the ditch, and continue straight on into a field at the top along the back of some cattle sheds then past a line of field maple and birch trees.

6. Once past the trees our path continues roughly along the middle of this field moving to the right closer to the hedge as the field narrows near the top. We cross a small wooden plank and pass alongside the stream before bearing right by an old log pile to reach a wooden stile alongside a metal gate.

7. Cross the stile into an open field where we continue along the left side. Numerous blue dragonflies provided some great entertainment as I passed along this stretch. At the end of the field we reach a track, which we follow up the slope to the right between two lines of overhead power cables.

8. At the top of the field carry straight on along the left hand hedge before continuing straight on towards a stile where the hedge bears left. Cross the stile over a small enclosure to another stile then diagonally right across another small enclosure to a fingerpost in the corner by another stile. We don't cross this stile; instead we turn back to the right up the left hand side of the enclosure that we've just crossed.

9. We leave the enclosure by yet another stile, continuing along the left hand hedgerow. Continue straight past the first

1. We start at the Norman Church of St Mary's, enthusiastically 'restored' in the Victorian era at the instigation of the daughter of the then Lord of the Manor to make it even more Norman than it apparently was. Despite this it's a very enjoyable building and worthy of further inspection. The churchyard was also largely extended around the same time demolishing several cottages and an Inn, which faced onto Newbury Road and giving the building it's almost cathedral like setting we see today. We cross Newbury Road towards the Crown Hotel where we turn left, past the Health Centre behind Priory House and along North Street. At the end, turn right along a tarmac footpath then left at the fork just after passing some metal bars. Further along, at a junction with other paths and where a redundant metal gate looks rather sad propped up against what has been a tremendously uninspired choice of fencing, continue straight on along the path and then over grassy scrubland to a wooden stile.

2. Over the stile we climb some steps to emerge on the side of the A339. Cross straight over when its clear, down some more steps on the other side and over another stile. Keeping to the hedge on the left, we cross another wooden stile in the top corner

Walk No. 12

stile where we enter the next field to another, which takes us through a narrow wood and over a second stile into the field beyond. Turn right in this field and follow along the hedgerow straight past a gap to another stile into the wood.

10. Cross the stile, over a small wooden bridge and along the path in the wood passing straight by the front of a rangers shed, over a gravel track and back onto the path by a marker post. After a while, the path curves to the left past a sign for Harridens Copse then comes to a gravel path where we turn right.

11. The gravel path doesn't stretch very far – at least not at the time of writing and ends at a ditch a short distance on. Continue along the path, taking the right fork at a junction a short distance on, keeping within the wood and after a while passing a metal gate on the right and then one on the left before the path passes into a field just to the right.

12. Continue straight on along the left hand hedge exiting in the corner alongside the cut-off trunk of a tree used as a marker post. Continue straight on, passing to the right of some tall elegant ash trees, straight on over a track and then along a long, clear winding woodland track.

13. We exit by a stile into a field, continuing straight on across the middle to another stile on the far side. Cross the stile and turn right along a grassy path crossing a second stile after a short distance to arrive back at the A339. Cross the road again carefully and turn right along the verge to pick up another footpath on the opposite side by lamppost number 004. We go down this path, across two small wooden bridges and over a stile to come into some scrubland. Turn right along the hedge until you come to a gate on your right with our path to the left. Follow this path out of the scrub and straight on onto a tarmac path.

14. Continue straight on at the end of the path across the intriguingly named Strokins Road and straight down Ash Grove, which becomes Love Lane and leads us out onto Ashford Hill Road. Here we turn right, to the old George and Horn – under restoration at the time of writing and the junction with the old Newbury Road.

15. Cross straight over towards the Fire Station turn left and take the narrow footpath, which runs beside it on its left past the

post box. Where this path opens out just after you've passed a white gate on your right, we turn right up a tarmac track that runs to the left of Eleven The Dell and up some steps straight on to bring us to the village recreation ground.

16. Our path is straight on keeping to the hedge on the right although the view is quite nice if you have the energy to walk up the hill to your left. Exiting by the large gate in the corner, we head straight on ignoring the path to the right follow this track down the hill and around to the right by Daisy Bank to emerge on Swan Street.

17. Swan Street has some of Kingsclere's oldest and finest architecture and numerous listed buildings, but I love the way some of its surplus commercial properties have been transformed into homes in recent years without loosing their essential character. What was Lloyds Bank at the junction on your left still carries the redundant supports, which held the banks name proudly aloft for many years and as we turn right and along Swan Street the old telephone exchange on the right still has its sign even if it is now emptied of the banks of relays and switches that enabled local citizens to connect with the outside world. Further along, the Swan Hotel is a far older building than its 18th century exterior suggests with a timber framed roof constructed in the mid 15th century.

Watership Down Inn, Freefolk

Built in 1840 as The Freefolk Arms, the Watership Down Inn started life as a tiny village alehouse and initially wasn't licensed to sell spirits. The village hasn't changed tremendously since then, but fame of the downs to the north has spread far and wide thanks to Richard Adams' wonderful book and the pub was renamed in honour of this in the mid-70's. The Inn is a Freehouse run by Mark and Alison Lodge who took over in 1993 and are proud to boast that throughout this time rabbit has never been on the menu! Thanks in no small part to the success of the novel, trade is much increased since the 1840's and the pub has been enlarged so that today there are two small bars, a large conservatory and an area known as 'the game's room' which features a pool table and a fascinating line-up of old penny-in-the-slot machines. There is a tiny garden with benches at the front, which was being re-paved and re-turfed at the time of my visit, and also a wonderful large garden to the rear with a magnificent children's play area. The line-up of real ales is ever-changing but includes one Mild, which was the Oakleaf Brewing Companies Maypole at the time of my visit. Alongside were Crouch Vale Brewery's Essex Blonde, Huffkin from the Ringwood Brewery and Stonewall from the York Brewery. Fresh food is available everyday during lunchtimes and evenings and I have to admit I particularly liked the sound of their Somerset Chicken - 'Breast of chicken in a creamy cider sauce with mushroom and apples, topped with cheese and bacon and served with fresh vegetables and croquette potatoes'. Slightly more local was Smoked Trout from the River Test accompanied by a full plate of freshly available seasonal leaves, cucumber, tomatoes, onions, beetroot, potato salad, coleslaw and French bread. Children are allowed in the conservatory and games room and of course are welcome in the garden.

The pub is open 11:30-15:00 and 18-23:00 Monday to Saturday, 12-15:00 and 19-22:30 Sundays. Food is available until 14:30 at lunchtimes and until 21:30 Monday to Saturday 20:15 Sunday.

Telephone 01256 892254

Walk No. 13

Approx. distance of walk: 8 miles. Start at OS Map Ref SU 492486.

Parking is available along Laverstoke Lane.

Where does the village of Laverstoke end and that of Freefolk begin? The answer is really in the late 18th century when Freefolk House and its grounds were enlarged and landscaped to become Laverstoke Park, displacing the few scant hovels that remained in Laverstock village and leaving only the tiny church of St Mary's to mark the spot. Though St Mary's was then nominally used as a mortuary chapel for the Portal family, it fell into slow decline and was all-but demolished in 1953 with its more notable monuments being moved to Hinton Ampner. Freefolk had started out as two settlements, Freefolk Priors in the northwest owned by the Priory of St Swithun's in Winchester and Freefolk Syfrewast in the southeast owned by the Syfrewast family. This was of course long before the Portal family came along and built their mill almost slap bang between the two and called it Laverstoke Mill just to confuse the issue. The Portal family were very benevolent employers and the cottages they built for their employees – such as those along Laverstoke Lane were far superior to anything that had gone before. Its not clear how great was their contribution towards the Victorian church of St Mary's, which superseded St Mary's in the park, but the large elaborate gate that once marked Laverstoke Parks private entrance into its grounds remains to tell its own story.

This walk takes us back past its start at point 9, so although it can easily be done as one long continuous walk, it's also easy to do as two separate walks which you may prefer particularly if you intend to look inside St Nicholas's Church. If you've walked the Whitchurch walk detailed elsewhere in this book, you'll recognise the short section that takes us past Bere Mill at point 12.

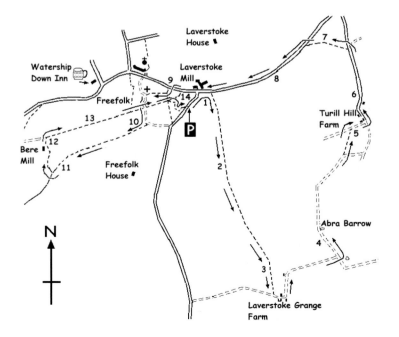

1. Start at the end of Laverstoke Lane opposite the fort-like entrance to Laverstoke Mill. Despite it's military appearance, the huge cannon ball like object stuck in the ground under the post box is not the aftermath of some forgotten conflict, rather an intriguing device said to have been installed to divert the wheels of heavily loaded wagons from accidental brushes with the brickwork when the mill was at its height. We head to the right along the footpath beside the B3400. Just past the end of the green corrugated metal fence on the left, our footpath goes off to the right where an old Post Office Telephones inspection hatch is set into the path.

2. The path runs alongside a field for a while before we head through a pine wood – in fact there's a bench here if you're already out of breath. We continue straight on and out of the wood following along the left hand hedgerow of a large field. There's a good view here over to the right where you get an occasional glimpse of the new Freefolk House.

3. Continue straight on through the hedge at the top of the field, straight over a grass track to continue now downhill along the edge of the next field. At the bottom of this field we move onto a grassy track heading towards a red brick house at Laverstoke Grange Farm. At the tarmac road just before this house we turn left to pass straight on through the old farmyard. We then turn left again where our path meets some trees down a gravel track past some tennis courts.

4. At the bottom of this track just past Pot Bottom Cottage (which takes its lovely name from the old name for the farm we passed a moment ago), we turn right and follow a pretty, grassy track between hedgerows. The track runs alongside a field before coming to a halt where a gravel track crosses our path. Several Lapwings paraded themselves in the field ahead where a notable patch just to the right marks the site of an ancient burial mound. We turn left up the track shortly passing a slightly less subtle barrow at the top of the hill. The OS map records this particular bump as Abra Barrow, but whether Abra is derived from the Latin for 'enormous tussock' or misnamed in tribute to a famous Swedish band; I simply did not have time to uncover before publication. Ignore the track right here, continuing straight on with a nice view over to the right over Turrill Hill Farm to Overton and beyond.

5. Keep on along the dirt track as it follows the hedge on the left, then after a downhill section where the dirt track turns sharp right, continue straight on along a grassy track towards the farm. We then turn right when we reach a footpath sign to take us along another track passing to the right of some heavily buttressed old brick and flint farm buildings. At the end of this track turn left along the tarmac road.

6. A wonderfully orangey-brown buzzard (at least I think that's what it was) swooped past just in front of me along here carrying some small black furry prize home for a light snack. There are pleasing views over to the left along here down into the little narrow valley before we reach the signpost for our footpath, which is off to the left over a stile.

7. This ancient path was once an alternative route between Dellands in Overton and Freefolk and becomes a much wider track as it continues on towards Overton in the east. Our route takes us west however, down into the little valley straight through a muddy gap in the hedge and then across the field on the other side clipping the hedgerow on the left before heading uphill towards a wooden gate on the far side.

8. We exit the field here over a stile and into a wood, turning right shortly to take us back to the B3400 where we turn left to follow the road back to Laverstoke. At the top of the hill along the way we pass two small abutments on either side of the road, which mark the point where a small wooden bridge carried hunting parties from Laverstoke House to Rotten Hill Copse and the more rural parts of the estate. A little further on we pass Church Lodge with Laverstoke House prominent behind. Here there was once a crossroads with the road north past the lodge taking us up to the old Laverstock village and the church of St Mary's.

9. Continue along the B3400 passing the Mill and Laverstoke Lane, crossing over shortly past the mill where the footpath ends on the south side. Just a little way further on, we cross back over to follow a signpost on the left into a field turning right as we enter the field to follow the hedgerow along.

10. At the end of the field we cross a stile out onto a track. A short diversion to the right here takes us to the rustic, simple little church of St Nicholas. The church is kept locked but details for obtaining the key are provided on the door and it is really the interior that's worthy of inspection with a

rather ornate and elaborate monument so its worthy of a return visit on another day. Return to the stile and continue past it on up the track. Pass by the drive to the cottages on our right and follow the track round to the left and uphill. At the top of the hill turn right through a gap into a field to follow the well-worn path along the top. There are very good views here back to the right of the old and the new Freefolk churches.

11. Until the 1930's, the woods to our left held a small square wooden tower, home to an elderly recluse by the name of Thomas Langhorne Foster. Although he was said to be harmless, he also wasn't very keen on visitors, and would welcome passers by who strayed to close with a loaded shotgun. Stay on the path and at the end of the field follow the track into the woods where you will see a stile shortly on the right. This takes us into another field where we follow the hedge as far as it goes on the left before turning sharp right downhill to a stile alongside a wall hidden behind some trees.

12. Cross the stile and follow the path alongside the roofed wall, and you'll emerge to the right of Bere Mill with a splendid view of the old bridge. Bere Mill started life as a corn mill and the sign on it that you might just be able to make out says 'This house and mill built by Jane, the widow of Tho Deane Esqr in ye year 1710.' Bere Mill was the location where the young Henry Portal, having secured its lease in 1712 began his company manufacturing high quality paper. Demand was such that by 1718, he had to move to the larger mill further upstream at Laverstoke. It was there in 1727 that he successfully negotiated a deal with a friend's uncle to supply banknote paper to the Bank of England, a contract so successful that it has continued uninterrupted to this day.

13. Follow the tarmac drive right past the old stables and then turn right through a wooden gate and straight on across a large field. Over a stile on the far side you'll find a bench beneath some oaks, which is a really lovely spot to sit and rest your weary limbs on a hot sunny day. Having summoned up your reserves for the final part of the walk, return to the standing position and continue straight on along the right hand edge of the field alongside a fence. At the end of this we pass through a gap between trees keeping to the right of a line of oaks and then straight on along the back of the cottages and across the track we went up earlier to pass through a gap into a field.

14. Here we head straight on towards the flagpole on top of Laverstoke Mill passing just to the right of magnificent Silver Fir. Over the crest, we head down to a stile turning right on the other side through a small garden with a wonderful sculpture and following the little gravel path down between the tennis courts and bowling green then left around the children's playground to return to Laverstoke Lane.

15. The pub is a short walk or very short drive from here along the B3400. If you're walking to the pub, don't miss the fabulous 'olde worlde' charm of Manor Cottages along the way. Built in 1939 by Lord Portal they are masterpieces of design and detail from the overindulgent thatch to the astounding front door hinges. Across the road Portals also laid out a now slightly neglected cross and garden for the people of Laverstoke and Freefolk in 1870. The stone cross had to be replaced with a wooden one some time ago and the water fountain beneath has also long run dry but the seat still works and you can stop and ponder its engraved missive 'Rest here awhile beneath the sign of love which tells thee of eternal love'.

The Gamekeepers, Mapledurwell

Having been the village pub for the best part of 200 years and given its rural location, its fair to say that many a pheasant plucker or his son will have supped his way through a pint or two in this cosy little hideaway, so although Mapledurwell's Inn was known for many years as the Queens Head, it does seem much more suited to its current guise as The Gamekeepers.

Phil and Sandra Costello are the current owners of this popular free house, which somewhat unusually plays host to koi carp in the original well inside.

Though these aren't on the menu, there is an otherwise extensive choice of dishes available from the normal bar snacks to full a la carte, all at very reasonable prices and with seasonal game an understandably popular choice. Ales on offer include Badger Best, Tanglefoot and Gribble's Fursty Ferret.

Opening hours are 11-23:00 six days and 12-22:30 Sunday with food available until 15:00 and then from 18-22:00.

Children and dogs are welcome.

Telephone 01256 322038

The pub is situated on Tunworth Road in Mapledurwell village

Approx. distance of walk: 7½ miles. Start at OS Map Ref SU 514688.

Limited parking is available along the Greywell Road or in the car park outside The Gamekeepers, but please let the landlord know that you'll be back to use the facilities!

I've left out one of Mapledurwell's most historical talking points from the main walk, although it's a relatively short distance from the pub either before you start or after you finish so you should take a look, this is of course the much celebrated infantryman originally painted at some time in the early 1800's on the wall of the farm at the entrance to the village along Tunworth Road. Legend has it that this was painted by a young soldier, the son of the farmer, to guard the farm while the son went off to fight in the Crimean war from which, sadly the son never returned. Less romantically is the tale that a businessman painted it as a form of relaxation while he was on holiday with relations who owned the farm. That the soldier's colourful form remains bright today is all thanks to his mysterious attendant who, as the elements have taken their toll and the soldier's origins have become hazier, drops by, unseen by all, to repaint and occasionally amend minor details to the bafflement of the entire village. Hopefully Mapledurwell's soldier will remain on watch over the village for many years to come so that future generations can ponder the legend and enjoy.

There were some fairly tall stinging nettles to contend with along section 3 of this walk so, unless you have Teflon knees or strong feelings about cruelty to plants, it may be as well to go prepared with a suitable bashing-stick. A compass may also prove handy to help navigate the unmarked paths across open fields.

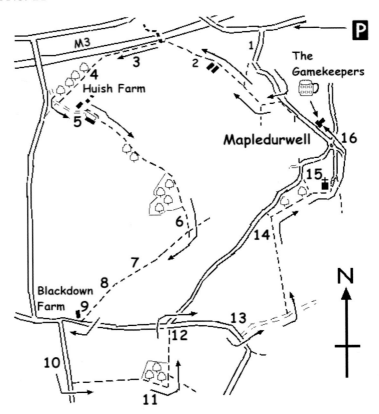

1. From the Gamekeepers, turn right up Tunworth Road. Then turn left opposite a white garage building, just before you reach Rye Cottage. Hiding round the corner here is a kissing gate into the field. Pass through the gate and turn right along the edge of the field.

2. At the top corner we cross a wooden stile which leads us into an open field, the footpath runs diagonally in a straight line across the field to the right from the stile, aiming for a mobile phone mast on the opposite side which is behind two metal barns. On reaching the barns, the path passes to the right around the outside of the barns continuing along a grassy strip on the far side, which leads towards the motorway.

3. There is a footbridge across the motorway at this point, but we don't cross it, instead continuing along the field edge on your right. Before you reach the corner of the field, the path heads off to the right along a narrow strip passing through a squeezer stile. Here our path runs briefly alongside a section of the Basingstoke Canal, unfortunately this now lies beneath the tarmac of the M3, so you will have to use your imagination.

4. After battling through the undergrowth and crossing over the Lyde River, we now pass over another stile before continuing along another narrow but much clearer strip between two barbed wire fences. The trees were particularly fine along this path and there is a very elegant field full of Poplars on the left before we reach a long row of mature Horse Chestnuts.

5. At the far end we reach a tarmac road where we turn left following the fingerpost across the bridge. Watercress beds take advantage of the pure spring water found at this point. Shortly up the hill, the path is diverted away from the main track at a point indicated by a fingerpost to the left. Here we

turn left then shortly right, continuing parallel to the track we've just left, shortly passing through a metal gate.

6. After passing a line of Beech trees and more Horse Chestnuts, we pass through a second metal gate at the top of the field. The path now leads through a lovely small copse. We emerge from the copse along the left hand edge of a field; here keep your eyes open for a tiny gap in the hedge on the left. Our path lies directly opposite this to the right, straight across the open field heading southwest.

7. If your aim is true, you should pass through the hedge on the opposite side alongside a marker post. This brings you to another large open field. The path was pretty vague here over a weedy and neglected field of Rape, but if you turn right along the field edge for about 5 yards then walk straight out into the field for the same distance, your path lies diagonally south west from this point passing slightly to the right of a wooden low-voltage electricity pole you can see ahead. This will bring you to a gap in the hedge alongside a rusting tractor-pulled rake.

8. Passing through the gap, we now walk diagonally to the left across the next field making straight for the near corner of the metal barn at the bottom of the hill. A pair of Lapwings circled noisily overhead as I made my way across.

9. At the barn, we turn left, at the time of writing passing over metal hurdles via a couple of handily placed pallets. Keep to the left of the farm buildings then beyond them turn right to take the track out through double metal gates and onto a country road.

10. Turn right along the road, down the hill to a junction with another road where we turn left. Up ahead in the distance a dozen-or-so gliders were a marvellous sight, twinkling in the sunlight as they circled for thermals high above Lasham airfield. Just after we pass the drive to Hackwood Farm on the right, you'll see our footpath sign on the left up the bank. Our path runs straight on across the field from this point towards the woodland you can see up ahead.

11. As you near the top of the field, you'll see the path passes to the right of the wood, through a wooden gate. Pass through the gate and along the left hand edge of the next field. Large patches of Foxgloves broke up the darkness beneath the trees on the left. Towards the top of the field just past a metal horse trough, we pass over a stile on the left alongside an Oak tree.

12. Our path continues along just inside the woods, straight past a stile on the right, until we reach the end of the wood where we come out over another stile alongside a wooden shed. Continue straight ahead following the right hand edge of the field down to the road. Although it was a very hot day when I researched this walk, I was still more than a little surprised to see clouds of smoke rising from the grassy track as I approached this point in the middle of nowhere without another soul for miles around! As I got closer, it was clear that the peaty ground was actually smouldering in several places, seemingly just about ready to burst into flames. Luckily I had my mobile phone and I'm pleased to say it only took about 10 minutes for the fire brigade to arrive and get things under control. It just goes to show you never know what you'll find out walking in the countryside!

13. Passing through the metal gate onto the road, we now turn right, continuing down a hill until we reach Ragmore cottage on the left where we take the byway alongside it off to the left. Follow this track for a short distance downhill keeping your eye open as we round a corner for a stile up into a field on the left.

14. Cross the stile and then proceed along the right hand edge of the field, continuing on as the path turns into a track and then passes out of the field. Down the bottom of a hill the track turns to the left past several pieces of redundant farm equipment, turn into the hedge over the right past a pile of old tyres and through a gap into the next field where the path continues along the left hand edge of the field.

15. A little further along the path turns into a track, we pass by a kissing gate and then down alongside a brick wall, which marks the boundary of St Mary's churchyard. The grey weatherboarded bell-turret lends an almost vaguely industrial air to this unfussy little church and although this particular part of the building is 17th century, hides what is thought to be one of the oldest bells in all Hampshire. Inside, enjoy the wonderfully simple ancient door latch and the lovingly preserved old weathervane, sad victim of a fairly recent storm.

16. We leave the churchyard by the main gate along the tarmac road, continuing left past the footpath sign and the first road junction from which you can see the Gamekeepers up ahead.

Walk No. 15

The Castle of Comfort, Medstead

Though the origin of Medstead's Castle may be conjectural, I'm pleased to record that the comfort on offer in the wonderful pub to which it gave its name is incontrovertible and several regulars were very happy to declare that Landlady Sue Wilson offers the best beer in the district in her welcoming 18th century Innspired House.

There are two bars in this friendly local and the service shines as brightly as the horse brasses that adorn their walls. It's not a food pub, but does offer ploughman's, toasties or jacket potatoes at lunch times with hotpots to warm you in the winter months. The special at the time of my visit was home made Lamb and Mint Kebab with French bread and salad at a price that would make you smile and you could wash this down with a pint of Courage or Usher's Best, Gales Butser or HSB. Children are allowed in the garden and play area outside and dogs on a lead.

Telephone 01420 562112.

The pub is in Castle Street Medstead.

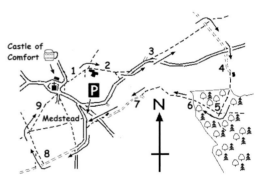

Approx. distance of walk: 4 miles. Start at OS Map Ref SU 658369.

Parking is available in the lay-by alongside the village green

Though today dwarfed by it's neighbour Four Marks just to the south, Medstead is by far the older of the two and many of the paths and tracks surrounding the village have been in use for centuries. An earthwork just to the north east of the village may have been an Iron Age fort, which somehow developed through local legend into the castle from which the pub and the villages Castle Street took their name. This is a short easy walk over good ground but it does involve quite a few stiles.

1. From the car park we walk north along Roe Downs Road onto the High Street and turn right onto Trinity Hill. Just after we pass the junction with Castle Street to the left, we take a narrow footpath on the right, not the one with the signpost, but another just to the left of the fence marked Squirrels. After a little narrow path, this takes us over a stile into a grassy field where we follow a path to the left passing to the left of the brick building ahead.

2. Alongside this building we find another stile, which we cross onto a concrete path shortly turning right to follow the path behind the building and through a small copse. We then cross another stile into small field keeping straight on across to another stile where we take the path to the left to bring us to a road.

3. Turn left along the road, passing Redwood Lane to reach a stile on the left. Cross over the stile and follow a well-trodden path across this field to the far right corner under a telephone mast. Here you'll find another stile onto a wide fenced off path.

4. At the end of this path another stile takes us onto a gravel track where we turn right, continuing straight on past a road junction onto the gravel bridleway indicated on the other side. This track weave left then right by some stables and the made-up track gives way to a narrower dirt path, which leads us into Chawton Park Wood.

5. As we enter the wood continue straight on for a few yards to a marker post where our path is the large one more or less straight ahead slightly to the right. The path goes downhill through the wood and emerges at a clearing where it meets other paths alongside a four finger post. Here we turn right along a grassy track.

6. After a nice wide path, we reach a junction where the path narrows, here we go left and almost immediately cross a low fence into a field heading straight on to pass just to the left of the large neat hedge directly before you. Keep straight on where you reach this hedge shortly to hop over the remains of a broken stile into the enclosure beyond where we follow the path sharp left.

7. We exit the enclosure over another stile then through a gate and straight on onto a very old track with small embankments on either side. Keep straight on and this will shortly lead you to the car park alongside the village hall where you can head right, back towards our starting point or continue on a short loop to bring you back nearer the pub. For this cross the road at the entrance to the car park onto a small tarmac path you'll find ahead slightly to the right alongside a children's playground.

8. Follow this path to bring you out onto South Town Road where we turn left staying on the left side around the sharp corner to the right until its safe to cross. Where the road turns left, we continue straight on along Homestead Road just after Sycamore Cottage. Follow this track till you reach a footpath on the right shortly after 'La Jonchere'. Our path continues straight on where we reach a field to pass through the large hole in the hedge you can see on the far side.

9. Through the hole, the path is diagonally to the right as indicated by the signpost towards a section of rusty metal fence you can see on the far side. Beyond this we continue in the same direction across another field to exit along a narrow path onto the High Street opposite the Church.

Half Moon and Spread Eagle, Micheldever

The unusual name of this pub dates back just over 150 years when a fire destroyed a pub known as the Spread Eagle which was just down the road. This pub was then known simply as the Half Moon. Following the fire the two landlords got together and well, you can guess the rest.

The age of the building isn't known, but the exposed section of wattle and daub in the main bar suggests that it goes well beyond that of its first recorded licence, which was issued in 1749. This is Greene King house ably run by the landlord and landlady Raymond Douglas and Belinda Boughtwood and it appears regularly in Good Beer guides. It's a warm friendly place with one main bar with a collection of unusual and obscure banknotes across the ceiling, there's a small games room and a separate dining area. There is also a large garden at the back with free entertainment provided by some free range bantams and the family guinea pigs.

Belinda is responsible for most of the fresh home-cooked food and the pubs motto 'We are not a fast food outlet, we serve good food as fast as we can.' Is as clear a statement as any that quality comes before all other considerations. Daughter Charlotte who happened to be scoffing her tea at the time also enthused about the high standard of Mum's cooking with an unprompted request for seconds of the Chicken Curry!

Popular dishes amongst the customers are the Steak Cob Rolls with rib-eye steak, mushrooms and onions and the Half Shoulder of Lamb with rosemary and redcurrant gravy. Charlotte also recommends the Chicken Tikka Bites with rhubarb chutney and the Moon Burger and Chips. As a Greene King house, there is only one guest ale – Everard's Tiger at the time of my visit alongside Greene Kings IPA, Abbot Ale and XX Mild, which seems to be growing in popularity. The blue Cask Marque plaque by the door testament that all of these will reach you in absolutely prime condition. Well-behaved children and dogs on a lead are welcome.

The pub is open 12-15:00 and 18-23:00 Monday to Saturday and 12-15:00 and 19-22:30 Sunday and food is available all the time.

Telephone 01962 774339

Approx. distance of walk: 4½ miles. Start at OS Map Ref SU 516391.

Parking is available alongside Micheldever recreation ground.

Sat plumb between the railway to the west and the old A33 trunk road to the east, Micheldever has remained a blissful old world village full of ancient (16thC) and really ancient (15thC) timber-framed thatched cottages happily bypassed by all and sundry. Even when they built the railway, they were thoughtful enough to put the station over 2½ miles away so not to disturb its rural tranquillity. Micheldever's 'unusual' octagonally centred church is notable not only for its remarkable Georgian extension - the beauty of which well and truly lies within - but also for the fact that almost twenty years ago villagers managed to raise the enormous sum of £70,000 between themselves to save its magnificent medieval tower, a noble feat worthy of a memorial in itself. This is a relatively easy walk with no stiles and only a couple of minor ascents to negotiate.

1. From the car park, we go west along Duke Street, turning right at the junction along Church Street, which brings us to St Mary's church. In the churchyard the body of 19-year-old Henry Cook lies in an unmarked grave. Henry was one of two martyrs of the agricultural 'Swing Riots' that took place in 1830 and while hundreds were transported for life as a result, he was hanged for knocking the hat from the head of a local MP. Unfortunately for Henry he was carrying a sledgehammer at the time and what the ploughboy claimed as accidental was construed as wilful intent to murder. Enjoy the

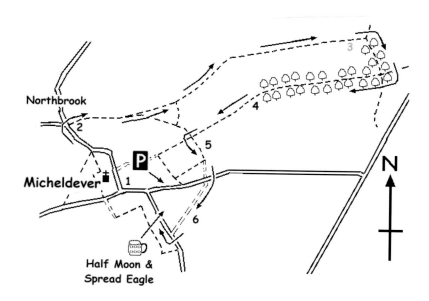

church; don't miss the gargoyles on its tower or the subtle way that extension is grafted on before exiting back onto Church Street heading left toward Northbrook past the triflingly ostentatious school clock tower.

2. As we reach this tiny hamlet, turn right along the signposted bridleway just by the road sign. We follow a well-trodden path straight up the field towards the hilltop. Pass through the metal gate at the top of the hill and then follow the trees on the left hand side along the top of the field.

3. On the far side of this field we pass through another metal gate then straight on along a grassy track. Passing by a derelict metal gate we come into an open field continuing straight on along the left hand hedgerow passing West Stratton Farm over on the left. We arrive at another metal gate, which we pass through and then turn right along a muddy bridleway.

4. At the top of a short climb, we reach a crossroads with another bridleway by a post and we turn right along this next track. Follow this track straight on for a mile or so, past junctions with other tracks eventually emerging onto an open path between fields with Micheldever village ahead to the left. Turn left where the next track crosses your path just before the end of the strip of woodland parallel to our path on the right.

5. This path, known locally as Chapel Avenue or more grimly Coffin Walk, links the churches of East Stratton and Micheldever and takes us back towards the village. After a while you will see the football pitches over on the right and as we reach the corner of this area we turn right to follow the track slightly to their left, which will bring us to the road.

6. Cross the road and carry straight on along the track beside the mustard coloured cottage. Following the track around to the right where the surface becomes grass. The track leads us round to Winchester Road opposite a row of small cottages where we turn right for a short distance to bring us to the pub.

The Mole, Monk Sherborne

Once known as the New Inn, The Mole is believed to be the only pub so named in the whole of England. Why did they change the name and why to The Mole? Well you'll have to dig deep to unearth that story and certainly Landlord Graham Titterton was not about to give me the scoop. There are two bars – The Mole Hole and The Mole Hill and a fine line-up of sculptural Moles dug-in behind the bar. Children and other Miners are welcome and dogs are allowed in the small garden and the public bar.

The food is varied and reasonably priced and two popular dishes are the Prawn Festival - with Tiger Prawns and Queen pink Prawns on a bed of Prawn Rice - and a Rump Steak so enormous that the staff feel obliged to point out that although it comes with chips and salad, it doesn't come with veg because there isn't room on the plate!

The Mole is open 12-23:00 Monday to Saturday and 12-22:30 Sunday with food available until about 21:00 every day.

Telephone 01256 850033

Walk No. 17

Approx. distance of walk: 5½ miles. Start at OS Map Ref SU 608567

Parking is available in car park to the rear of the village hall.

What put the Monk in Monk Sherborne? Well this walk will show you, taking in as it does the remains of the Benedictine priory sited just up the road at Pamber End. What put the End in Pamber? Well that's a whole other story. The marshy section at point 9 means water-resistant footwear is recommended for this walk even in summer.

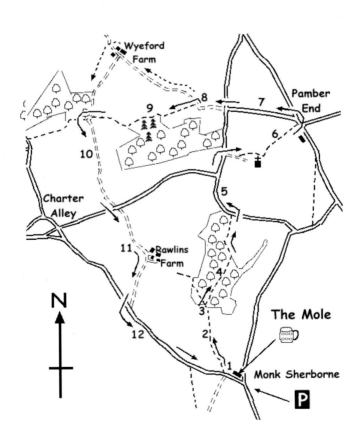

1. From the front of the pub, turn right along the road towards Charter Alley for a short distance, then turn left between Carlyle House and Sunnyside to follow a narrow grassy footpath.

2. Just round the corner, we cross over a stile and then at the end of this short, grassy section another stile that takes us into a field. Over the stile we turn left continuing in the same direction as we had been following the left hand edge of the field to the right of a line of trees.

3. At the bottom of the field we cross another stile and then once into the field continue again in the same direction as previously in a line about 15 yards away from but parallel to a small copse on the left. At the bottom of the field this brings us to the start of a short line of oaks that run parallel to a chicken wire fence. Continue straight on between the fence and the trees. At the point where the fence heads off to the left, we pass into the woods alongside a marker post.

4. Just inside the woods, take the path diagonally off to the right marked on the large oak tree. Following a clear trail through the woods. There are some marshy bits here, but they are very easy to negotiate around. At the end of the woods, we cross a firebreak then into a field where the sight of the Priory Church greets us more or less straight ahead. Turn left following along the edge of the field.

5. We leave this field in the bottom corner passing between two oak trees to join a narrow road. Turn left along the road shortly passing over a little bridge where the contractor and surveyor have been proudly recorded for posterity on the blue brick crown posts. Continue on past the school and then turn left between the white palings that border the gravel drive to the 12th Century Priory Church. Our path crosses the stile you'll see shortly on the left, but its well worth a short diversion to see the outside of the church – sadly the inside is closed unless you obtain the keys by prior arrangement.

6. Return to cross the stile and follow the path to the right around the edge of the cemetery. At the end of the open meadow, the path turns left along a narrow strip of woodland before crossing a little wooden bridge. This brings us out into a field where we head diagonally, just to the right of our previous course. When you reach the brow of the hill, head for a gap in the middle of the trees that lie between red brick buildings on the right and grey farm buildings on the left.

7. Assuming your course was true, you should pass through a gap that brings you out onto the A340. If it's a particularly warm day you might want to stop for a beer at the Queens Collage Arms just a few yards down the road on your right, otherwise turn left and then left again along Ramsdell Road.

8. Follow the straight part of this road to the junction where the main road turns left. We continue straight on up the gravel drive to Wyeford ignoring the sign that says 'Private Drive – No unauthorised vehicles'. Follow the drive as it curves round to the right past the entrance to Clapper Hill Bee Farm then take the footpath on the left marked with a post, just to the right of the drive of Little Holm.

9. After a relatively straight section, the path weaves around to the right following the edge of the wood. Its clear the path here could be quite marshy after heavy rain and even though the weather had been dry around the time of my walk, a wooden plank stopped short of clearing the worst section. You may need to make a diversion along the route through Wyeford Farm if things look really bad. After clearing the marsh we come to a wooden bridge and stile. Cross the stile and turn right to follow the path under the trees.

10. Keep going to the top of the field where the path leaves the trees alongside a white metal gate with a stile beside it. Cross the stile and the ditch beyond then turn left along the green track. Ignore the stile and gate straight ahead and continue left along the track. After a while we pass around the side of a white metal gate continuing straight on afterwards then turning slightly left where the footpath gives way to a gravel drive.

11. Reaching a road at the end of the drive we turn left then immediately right up another gravel drive and onto the grassy footpath beyond. Follow this path until you reach a tarmac track alongside Rawlins Farm. Here turn right and continue right along the tarmac drive.

12. At the junction with the road, cross over and turn left and follow this road back to the pub.

Walk No. 17

The Red Lion, Water End

Traffic swoops past the Red Lion these days at considerably higher speeds than it did in the old turnpike era, when a tollgate that stood alongside helped more than a little to encourage thirsty travellers to take a break from their trip along the dusty main road to London.

Though Landlord Peter Miles can no longer offer you good stabling or a change of horses, he otherwise continues the tradition of hospitality passed on by his antecedents, with thirst-quenching ales and a range of reasonably priced pub food to entice the weary traveller, particularly recommending his home-made Steak and Ale pie for any ravenous walkers who traipse the paths hereabouts.

This unpretentious little pub is owned by Courage as part of their Unique Pub Company group and the current building dates back 200 years or more. Though it doesn't boast ghostly highwaymen or spectral apparitions, Peter is convinced a small corner behind the bar does play host to a mischievous gremlin as items left in one particular spot are prone to disappear, reappearing mysteriously several weeks later in a completely different location, a paranormal occurrence that is said only occasionally to coincide with visits from his grandchildren. Talking of raised spirits, the stalwart Courage Best is always happily on tap alongside Adnams and other guest ales such as Greene King and London Pride.

Children are welcome, but dogs on a lead at the benches outside please.

The pub is open seven days a week. No food on Mondays, but every other day its available until 21:30.

Telephone 01256 762675

Walk No. 18

The pub is situated on the A30 Basingstoke to Hook road about 1½ miles east of Old Basing.

Approx distance of walk: 6½ miles. Start at OS Map Ref SU 699522.

There is space to park in the lane just before and after Brick Kiln Canal Bridge and also near the junction along the Greywell Road, alternatively there is a lay-by on the eastbound carriageway of the A30 just after Water End (SU 696532) from here you can walk east and start the walk where we've crossed the road at point 10

Nately Scures and Up Nately are tiny gems hidden right on Basingstoke's doorstep. Thousands of cars pass nearby on the A30 and the M3 without ever being aware of their existence, which is probably a good thing – tucked away here are two truly wonderful churches along with the western end of the Basingstoke Canal - built with high hopes and ambitions over two hundred years ago, this now rather forlorn stretch hasn't seen a barge within living memory, it survives as a tranquil, glorious ruin remote from it's industrial origins, as worthy of our adoration as any castle, stately manor or prehistoric tump. Nately Scures is shown on some old maps simply as Skewers, which seems a very reasonable guide to its correct pronunciation. The name is said to be derived from one-time owners the de Scures family who originated in the Escures region of Calvados. Owners of OS Explorer map 144 who do not possess very long arms or a degree in paper-folding will recognise this as one of the most difficult walks to navigate in this book.

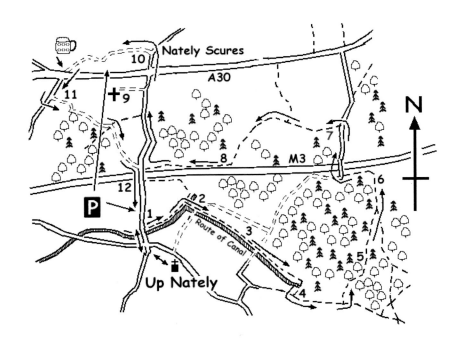

1. Take a quick look over the parapet of the bridge before we start; it helps to grasp both the amount of work that went into building the canal and also to appreciate its current state of decline. We cross the bridge to the junction with the Greywell Road passing a primordial swamp on the right that looks on the verge of spawning new life-forms, turn left and just down the road on the right you'll find the beautiful church of St Stephen with a fine wrought iron gate and fabulous boot-scrapers. Largely rebuilt in 1844, this delicate confection, its battlemented tower almost overwhelmed by the nave, includes a glorious Norman doorway and an interior that delights in its simplicity. Having inspected the church, we return to the canal bridge.

2. Go down the steps beside the bridge near the white handrail. These take us down to the old canal towpath where we turn left to pass under the bridge. Depending on the time of year and the water level in the canal, the aromatic mud may avail you with its delicate bouquet and clearly the waterfowl that enjoy this section are not endowed with our sense of smell. Shortly, we turn across a small footbridge to the right, bypassing the siding for the old Brickworks and continuing along the towpath under Slade's Bridge. A handy display board here explains the history of this particular section.

3. The anvils of numerous thrushes' glint along this section of path, surrounded by smashed and discarded snail shells. We pass under Eastrop Bridge where you can see the corners bitten deep by the ropes where horses once dragged the barges past this point. The further on we walk, the more the canal becomes beautifully untamed and before long even the water gives up its fight against the onslaught of nettles. Here our path veers slightly to the right uphill and away from this little trodden end of the towpath. We pass along a colonnade of tall oaks up a permissive path, shortly turning right to cross over the unseen western portal of the Greywell tunnel. A display board tells of how the tunnels misfortune has accidentally led it to become one of the most important sanctuaries for bats in the UK.

4. Continue over the portal and up the slippery bank where the path splits temporarily into a myriad of alternative routes. Any will do as they converge again at the top of the slope where we turn left along a bridleway. We follow this with woodland on our left and a thin hedge to our right with an open field behind - where this field ends and we reach woodland on our right, we turn left following the arrow on a marker post along another footpath.

5. This footpath runs in a straight line, passing a water-filled sinkhole on the right formed where the tunnel roof collapsed far beneath. We cross a plank over a ditch continuing straight on up a steep and much wider track. After pausing for breath at the top, follow the path indicated by a direction arrow on the post to the right, shortly turning left off this mud track onto a grassy track where a sign ahead along our original route warns 'Private – No Public Right of Way'.

6. We now continue straight on for some way, ignoring a muddy track that crosses our path shortly along one of the finest woodland trails I've walked in the area, we cross a small muddy ditch before reaching a wide clearing again keeping straight on and ignoring the track that veers off to the right. Soon we approach the motorway although that fact is only clear from the noise, not because it ever comes into sight. We continue straight on though the track veers sharp left and we shortly reach a fence separating us from the motorway bank where we also turn left.

7. Continue along this path by the fence till it exits onto a narrow road, here we turn right and cross the bridge over the motorway. There's a good view over to Basingstoke here if you can ignore the bloody great road beneath you. Continue along past the telephone masts till you see a footpath sign on the left. Pass through the metal gate into the field where we follow the direction indicated by the signpost diagonally across the field to the left, clipping the protruding hedgerow in the middle on our right as we make our way across to the opposite side of the field. When you reach the far side, turn left along the fence to a stile in the far corner.

8. Follow the path straight on over the stile following a well-trodden path in the wood. Ignore the arrow on a tree stump indicating a route to the left, instead follow the clear path straight on with a raised bank on your left, shortly crossing over a ditch and then continuing straight on past another arrow on a stump on the left. We then cross over two small ditches to reach the fence alongside the motorway. Turn right along the fence for a way then across a ditch and a stile into a small field. Ignore the lurid 'Private - Beware of Animals they bite' sign,

Walk No. 18

but clearly proceed with caution if you see large shadows moving in the trees. We exit the field by another stile on the far side, up some steps and under the Armco barrier to a road at the top.

9. Turn right along this road and shortly through the trees to the west you get a brief glimpse of the tiny church at Nately Scures. Continue along the lane until you see the signpost to St Swithun's on the left and make your way to the church. This simple Norman treasure is host to many delights such as the otherwise unremarkable memorial slabs on the north wall, which are all shaped to resemble the suites in a pack of cards – a good deal from the mason perhaps? Several stories surround the origins of the famous mermaid on the door pillar – replaced in 1968 to avoid further erosion with the original now safe inside the church. The anchor on the arch above must clearly have had some connection, but what about the unknown mariner whose tomb in the churchyard is also surmounted by a large anchor? Time has certainly stopped in more ways than one for a lonely Victorian pillar, once host to a notable sundial, which stands almost hidden in the far corner of the churchyard, in shadow now on even the brightest days. The small enclosure along the farm track nearby proved almost as entertaining as the church on my last visit with one of the sheep giving a ride to three chickens - all at the same time. Return to the main road and continue north to cross the A30. It's a dual carriageway at this point but relatively easy to cross providing you stop in the middle and keep looking the right way!

10. Continue along the lane on the opposite side for a short distance before turning left along the signposted byway. Ignore the turnings off into fields, continuing along the main track under the height barrier. There is a ford along this track but it does have a footbridge alongside, other muddy sections are also easy to avoid.

11. The track brings us out onto the A30 again, and a few hundreds yards down the road to the right is the pub. After refreshment, we once again cross the A30 with care, to proceed down Andwell Lane opposite. After about 100 yards take the bridleway signposted off to the left known as Coop Lane. This starts as a gravel track and narrows briefly as we pass the first section of woodland. Ignore the path off to the right along here and the kissing gate to the left as

the track bears right at a muddy corner, keep going until you reach a minor road at the top of a short slope.

12. Turn right along this road and cross the bridge over the motorway. If you fancy a challenge on the other side of this bridge to the left is a jungle-like footpath through swamps, which will take you back to the Brickworks siding on the canal, but I'd only recommend this for the more ambitious walker! Continue along the road to return to our starting point at the canal bridge.

The Globe on the Lake, New Alresford

All roads may once have led to Rome, but it's said that at the time The Globe on the Lake was founded, all travellers would pass through Alresford on their journey, hence the symbolic Globe of all nations. Whether or not this is true, this 17th century coaching inn situated on the edge of Old Alresford Lake is tremendously popular both for its extensive menu and for the restful, ornithological wonderland that can be viewed from it lakeside garden, where birds of all nations do pause from migrations to enjoy the waters of the lake.

Owned by the Duveen Conway family, The Globe offers an extensive menu of freshly prepared food using local produce, a wide and varied selection of beers and what they describe as a 'challenging' Wine List. It has been recommended by Mark Oaten MP for its good food and was winner of the Real Fire 'Pub of the year' award in 2002.

The pub is open 11:00-15:00 and 18:00-23:00 Monday to Saturday and 12:00 to 15:00 and 19:00 to 22:30 Sunday though this is extended to all day opening during the summer months.

Children are welcome in garden, dining and garden rooms for lunch and early suppers, Dogs in the garden on a lead.

Telephone 01962 732294

The pub is at the northern end of New Alresford along the B3046 Basingstoke road.

Walk No. 19

Approx. distance of walk: 5 miles. Start at OS Map Ref SU 588340.

Parking is available at the northern end of Old Alresford Green either in the lay-by along the B3046 parallel to Christy Hall or on the verge north of Green Close.

Before the Great Weir was built to control the waters at the end of the 12th-century, the lands in the upper Itchen valley where it met the Tichborne and Candover streams were largely impassable. So it was that the dry route from the Anglo-Saxon capital in Winchester to the town of Alton and beyond ran far north of today's A31, crossing the waters at the two ancient settlements of Abbotstone and Alresford along the route of this walk. The Great Weir was built by Bishop de Lucy of Winchester who at the same time established a new market town just to its south as a speculative financial venture for the church. All three settlements struggled with various catastrophes in the years that followed, but the combination of the Black Death, the 'drying out' of the lands at the head of the Itchen and growing traffic to the southerly town led to the abandonment of the village of Abbotstone some time in the mid 16th century. As business in the 'New' part of Alresford boomed it quickly outgrew its northerly ancestor (which thus became 'Old'). Subsequently the head of the river Itchen was renamed the Alre in honour of the towns and the Tichborne stream became the River Itchen to bring us the scene pretty much as we see it today! This walk starts and ends in Old Alresford from where after our walk we drive a mile south to the pub in New Alresford, crossing the Great Weir along the way.

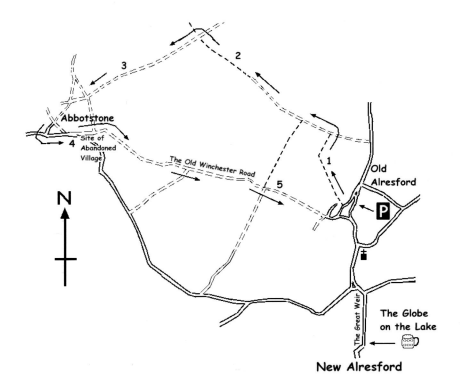

66

1. From the lay-by, walk towards the southern end of the green along the tarmac road that fronts Christy Hall. Take a narrow path off to the right between the houses called Glenmead and Timber Cutters and go straight across the open area at the top, along a tarmac path and then up the narrow path between fences alongside the water treatment plant. Continue straight on, northwest across the field here to a stile at the far side. Its well worth pausing when you reach the stile to take in the view back over the houses and churches of both Old and New Alresford.

2. Over the stile the path turns sharp right along the hedgerow exiting this field through a gap in the hedge. Turn left at this point uphill along a track passing to the left of a large corrugated-iron farm building. There are excellent views all round from the top of the hill. Just over the crest, we pass through a hedge then down the left side of a field to a track at the bottom, which is an old droving road known today as the Oxdrove way.

3. Turn left along the track, passing some semi-derelict farm buildings and along the edge of a field known as Lower Walk Field. Continue straight on past the exit to this field turning left at the signpost just before the metal gate. The notable embankment in the field to the right dates from the 17th century when a very large brick-built Italianate-style house stood slightly behind it to the northeast. Constructed by the 1st Duke of Bolton, it is said to have once entertained Queen Anne and to have had over 100 rooms, however it was never completed and was abandoned in favour of the original Hackwood House, which the Duke built near Basingstoke. The house is long gone, but you can enjoy the delicious little dovecote atop the farm building on its site.

4. The track becomes a metalled road after a short distance and we continue straight on to a T-junction where we join the old Winchester road. Turning right here for a short distance brings you to the original river crossing and a pleasant view of the meandering Candover stream, however we turn left, up the hill to the site of the medieval village of Abbotstone. Where the road bears right, we leave the tarmac to follow what was the original road along the track straight on. A few yards across the field, just to the right of the junction stood the village church in its churchyard and the lumps and bumps further ahead show where other tenements stood long ago. Ignore the path straight on into the field you reach shortly, bearing right to continue along this grand old track with its dense hedgerows on either side.

5. Ignore another track off to the right shortly and carry straight on at a crossroads where the only right of way indicated is to the right. Shortly you reach a tarmac road, which brings us back to Old Alresford village green.

The Bolton Arms, Old Basing

Like many of the older buildings in the village, parts of The Bolton Arms were built with bricks salvaged from the ruins of Basing House taken at the behest of Oliver Cromwell. Whether or not this has anything to do with the friendly ghost said to pass through the snug bar on occasion in full Cavalier regalia is open to speculation. Certainly numerous colourful characters must have graced this hostelry during its 400-year history and I'm sure many of them would be more than happy to return to it as their favourite haunt. Landlords Nick and Joanna Bell keep an open mind about such things but I'm sure their delicious home cooking will encourage warm spirits in anyone. Tempting treats vary from the simple – Three Speciality Sausages with Onion Gravy and Vegetables of the day or The Bolton's Steak, Mushroom and Red Wine Pie with Sauté potatoes and Vegetables. To the sophisticated – Venison braised in a red wine, redcurrant and cranberry sauce with diced ham, onion and mushrooms or perhaps Spicy Baked Trout; a whole oven baked trout marinated in lime and paprika, stuffed with onion, red pepper and mushrooms and served with new potatoes and vegetables. As well as a full lunch and evening menu, sandwiches and baguettes are available at lunch times and there's a Traditional Roast on Sundays. Being a Freehouse, Nick likes to have a variety of real ales on tap and alongside Courage Best and the Dark Mild favoured by his regulars I found Porky and Best from the Hampshire Brewery and Good Old Boy from the West Berkshire Brewery at the time of my visit, shortly to be replaced by the memorably-titled Piddle-in-the-hole from the Piddle Ywre Brewery in Worchester! The Bolton Arms is a relatively small pub so dogs are only allowed in the large garden at the back.

The pub is open 11:30-14:30 and 17:30-23:00 Monday to Friday, 18-23:00 Saturday and 12-15:00 Sunday (also some Sunday evenings during the summer). Lunch is available 12:15 to 14:00.

Telephone 01256 322085

Approx. distance of walk: 7miles. Start at OS Map Ref SU 668534

Parking is available in the car parks at the recreation ground and in Riley Lane.

Despite its location on the cusp of Basingstoke's bulging nether regions, Old Basing has managed to retain a physical and spiritual independence from its neighbour; adopting a very cavalier attitude to any hint of amalgamation.

1. From the Bolton Arms we take the signposted footpath along Riley Lane opposite. Continue straight on along the tarmac past the allotments and onto the dirt track beyond the cemetery.

2. Where you reach what appears to be a junction in the track, keep going to the left passing a telephone mast. Do not cross the footbridge ahead, instead turn left and over the stile beside the metal gate along a wooded path.

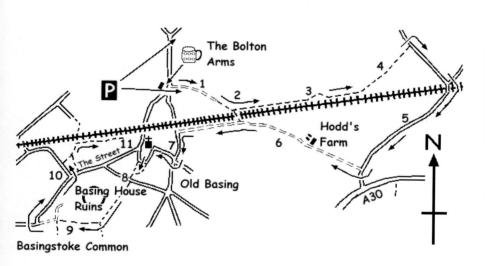

3. The path is quite clear along here and though it does become marshy in places it was quite easy to walk around these parts. Before long we reach a stile that leads us out of the wood to continue into a grassy field with the hedgerow on our right. Here a newly born calf and its mother blocked my path and I had to detour through the woods. I probably arrived for the best bit, watching from a respectful distance as the little calf spent the best part of twenty minutes struggling to her feet. Assuming you don't have to accommodate such detours, continue straight on to cross a stile at the top of the field, and then turn right to bring us back alongside the course of the railway.

4. Towards the end of this field, there were again some easily avoided marshy spots just before a metal gate into the next field. Passing through the gate, keep now to the left hand edge of the field up to the top corner. Here we pass through a big blue metal gate and onto a dirt track on the other side.

5. Turn right along the tarmac road at the end, keeping right over the railway bridge at the top of a short hill. The road passes alongside woodland on the left for a distance and you get a magnificent view over the woods to the east as we head downhill. Shortly after we leave the wooded section, we turn right along a concrete and then tarmac track towards Hodd's Farm.

6. Continue straight on through the farmyard and past the lovely old farmhouse, a little further along we pass by a footbridge over the railway, which you might recognise as the one we passed earlier. Again don't cross over the bridge, but continue along the track passing through a lovely little woodland dell only slightly marred by the occasional discarded bathtub.

7. At the road, turn left, shortly passing canal house at the point where we pass otherwise imperceptibly over the route of the Basingstoke Canal. At the junction by the carnival bench opposite the school, turn right down church lane crossing the canal route once again but this time slightly more noticeably. Turn left as you come to the church and carry straight on along a narrow gravel path that runs in front of Whitegates.

8. Turn left when you reach the junction with another path, crossing the road at the end and continuing straight on across the car park of the Old Basing British Legion Club, through a short wooden gate and over a stile. Follow the path along the right hand side of the field and then over another stile at the top end continuing along the field edge.

9. We're now out on Basingstoke Common, follow the hedgerow as it curves round to the right and the towers of Basingstoke will come prominently into view ahead. As you start to come down the hill, head towards the metal gate with the tarmac road beyond. Pass through the interesting little gate and then cross the stile to the right onto the tarmac road where we turn left up the hill.

10. At the junction turn right across the old canal bridge. Shortly, through the hedge on the right you can see a long stretch of garden wall with an octagonal dovecote at one end and an octagonal summerhouse at the other, one of the few parts of Basing House to survive the siege by Cromwell's troops. Cross over when you reach the junction with 'The Street' and turn left down Basing Road. Next we turn right along a footpath just before we reach the bridge and almost immediately over to your right you'll see the ancient Grange barn, part of a riding stable until the civil war, then the scene of fierce fighting, it emerged remarkably unscathed from this fierce conflict, though it does bear the scars of one or two cannon balls!

11. Follow this path alongside the River Loddon, and then take the path off to the right, just before you reach the railway viaduct. At the end of the path, continue straight on along the tarmac road towards a thatched cottage at the end. Here we cross straight over the road ahead up the path with the green metal handrail, which brings us to the glorious church of St Mary's Old Basing with its rather quirky bench made up of old tombstones. This fine church is worthy of a long detour and inspection, but if you're pressed for time, we'll make a simple circumnavigation to enjoy the various gargoyles, which should promise enough to make you want to visit again.

12. Exit the churchyard to rejoin 'The Street' and continue right under the railway bridge passing the garage, the old Methodist chapel and the famous topiary at the end of Milkingpen lane to return to the Bolton Arms

The White Hart Hotel, Overton

Situated at the main crossroads in the village, parts of this historic building date back to the 15th century including the huge inglenook fireplace, which dominates the lounge bar. As well as its venerable age, the White Hart is also one of very few pubs in England that can boast having minted its own coins, with which local farmers could guarantee the loyalty of travelling herdsmen during the village's famous sheep fairs in the 18th century. Much enlarged and expanded during the coaching era, The White Hart saw off a younger rival 'The New Inn' which stood almost directly opposite during this period and nowadays is a Freehouse, which has been owned and managed by Bob Bush for the last 18 years. Bob's wife Pao is from Thailand and the popularity of the occasional Thai dish she was including in amongst the pub's traditional English menu has recently convinced them both that 'Pao's Thai Kitchen' is the way forward for the pub's restaurant. Whilst perhaps not the easiest of dishes to pronounce, such exotica as Kai Pad Met Ma Movng (sliced chicken stir fried with cashew nuts, mushrooms and onion) and Pla Rad Prik (crispy whole trout topped with special Thai sauce) have gone down an absolute storm with both locals and visitors alike and though the usual line-up of sandwiches, baguettes, ploughman's and jacket potatoes remain on hand for the traditionalist, why not try Pad Ta Lay (medley of mixed seafood in spicy sauce with lemon grass, basil and red pepper) or See Krong Mu Tod (pork ribs marinated with garlic and pepper) just for a refreshing change. Bottled Thai beer is available, or you may prefer Gales H.S.B, Fuller's London Pride or the Wychwood Brewery's Hobgoblin There are two bars and a restaurant area and also a large garden at the rear, which backs onto the River Test.

The White Hart Hotel is open 11-23:00 Monday to Saturday and 12-22:30 Sunday. Food is available Lunchtime and early evenings until 20:45.
Telephone 01256 770237

Walk No. 21

Approx. distance of walk: 7½ miles. Start at OS Map Ref SU 515496

There is generous free parking available on either side of Winchester Street and in the car park signposted off the B3400. This walk can be very wet underfoot particularly in section 5 near the source of the Test.

Overton never quite enjoyed the prosperity of Whitchurch, its near neighbour and long-time friendly rival. Like Whitchurch, Overton once boasted a silk mill whilst the coaching trade bought two hotels to Overton against Whitchurch's one. However Overton's silk mill failed and was gone, along with one of the hotels by the 1860's leaving agriculture with the regular sheep fairs, and Portals paper mill in Laverstoke as the chief employment of the village until Portals opened their Overton Mill in 1921. The large hotel site on the corner was eventually filled by the national school and its playground - now the village library and community centre – in which I remember spending many happy hours as an infant. Several shops which dominated village life through much of the last century have gone since then – Hides Department Store, Howard's newsagents and Gall's the butchers to name just three, but the site of all of these are at least still shops – a graphic illustration if any were needed of the strength of Overton's thriving community today.

Should you choose to visit St Mary's Church while you are in the village, see if you can spot the horses' teeth hidden amongst the flint work.

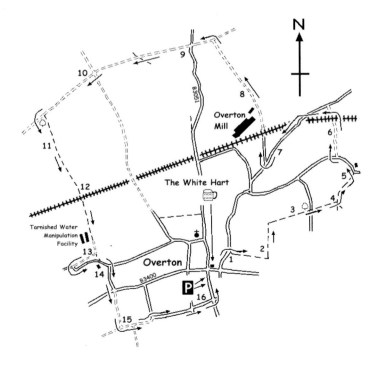

1. Starting at the White Hart, head east towards Overton Hill and then turn left down Station Road. Continue along here until you see a footpath sign on the right just before the grey tower of the Fire Station. Turn right at the top of the short slope along a tarmac path behind the houses then turn left through a metal gate marked with a yellow HCC footpath arrow.

2. Follow the well-defined footpath straight ahead uphill across the open field. At the top of the hill, pause for a breath and look back at the view over St Mary's Church and the wealth of trees in Overton's little valley. We turn left here, downhill along the field boundary marked by telegraph poles towards the dominating structure of Overton Mill.

3. At the bottom of the hill, the path forks left towards houses or right across open fields. We go right here to follow a sparse hedgerow for 100yards then straight on across the open field to a distant stile just to the right of a great Beech tree.

4. Cross the stile and the minor road to follow the path signposted straight across the field on the other side. Shortly we drop down a steep slope to face one of the uppermost stretches of the River Test. Continue down to the waterside fence where we turn left.

5. We pass the first footbridge but take the second a short distance further on alongside a ford. Follow this waterlogged track until you come to a metalled road directly in front of Polhampton Farm where we turn left along the road.

6. After a short distance, just past the first group of houses and before the second, we turn right along a gravel track. Just after we pass under the railway bridge, turn left up the bank and through the metal gate at the top (remembering to close it behind you!) here we follow alongside the railway line through the newly established David's Wood to the gate at the top end.

7. Passing through the gate we meet a minor road where we turn left following the road for about a quarter mile over the railway bridge and downhill – remembering to keep right if any cars approach. Shortly we come to a junction with another road where we turn right towards Overton Mill.

8. Follow the road under the railway bridge and then take the gravelled track that runs to the right of the gatehouse and the left of the car parks. This track takes us up and past the mill out into a green and more pleasant landscape.

9. Eventually you come to a T-junction with another track, which is the ancient drovers road known as the Harroway. Here we turn left following what I always think of as the M3 of the dark ages and where thousands of cattle and sheep were once herded to markets across the south. At the junction with the road, follow the Byway sign more or less straight across. Tracks made by 4WD vehicles loop off on either side here but lead nowhere so stick to the middle track downhill.

10. After a mile or so of this wonderful old wooded track, you reach a crossroads with another track where we continue straight on – Although you could take a short cut here back to the village. Another $\frac{1}{2}$ mile further on and you'll find a small but well-defined pathway off to your left around a large oak. There is a marker post here, but it was quite well hidden at the time of my visit.

11. Follow the path down the left hand side of the field alongside a magnificent ancient hedgerow. At the bottom of the field we continue more or less straight on either following the yellow marker arrow through the hedge along the official route or shimmying right through the big gap where the farmer drives his tractor. At the bottom of the field follow the path where it cuts into the hedge on the left by a marker post.

12. Follow the narrow path within the hedgerow weaving between the trees until you reach a stile. Over the top of this you'll find the '49 Steps', taking us down and across the railway line. The rails are not electrified here and providing you follow the instructions to Stop Look and Listen, it is easy to cross in relative safety.

13. Up the steps on the other side and over another stile, our path continues downwards shortly passing the picturesque Overton Water Treatment Works (well it all has to be done somewhere), continue along the gravelled track swinging around to the right down to the junction with Northington Farm Road at the Lynch.

14. Here we turn left, following a small channel of the Test that was a favourite spot for paddling in the 1960's. The area on your left once held several small cottages, but most were demolished in the 1950's. Shortly we pass Southington Mill, used as a corn mill until the 1930's when it was closed in controversial circumstances. Shortly afterwards it was turned into a private residence with a new wing added by the famous architect Sir Edwin Lutyens. At the junction of

Walk No. 21

Silk Mill Lane, turn right. There is a beautiful view of the Test from the small bridge although trees now obscure what was an even more picturesque view of Southington Mill. Further along the lane old watercress beds on either side have been attractively landscaped into private gardens.

15. Continue to the junction with the B3400, Thatched Tithe Cottage on the corner opposite was rebuilt from near total destruction after a devastating fire in the 1980's. Go straight across into Vinn's Lane, past the houses on either side and onto the track at the end. At the junction with another track at the top of the climb turn left and then keep left where we meet another track a short way further on.

16. At the junction with road by the house with the antlers, go right along Dellands. Straight over the crossroads and down Greyhound Hill to return to Winchester Street. Turn left to return to the Community Centre.

The Purefoy Arms, Preston Candover

I'm sure the venerable Admiral Purefoy; a local landowner who's family financed the building of this pub in the 1860's and who's crest became it's symbol, would have saluted the many improvements that have taken place at the Purefoy in the short space of time that it's been in the hands of the cheerful and enthusiastic partnership of Yvonne and John Culverwell and Karen and Steve Boyle. Inside, this spacious former hunting lodge is bright and airy but does include large open fires to warm the walker on cooler days. In the sunshine a huge garden at the back is equally welcoming and includes a children's play area - assuming they have any energy left to play at the end of your walk!

An excellent range of reasonably priced home-cooked food is available including a full a la Carte menu and a terrific Sunday lunch for only £6.95. Guest ales vary with Adnam's, HSB and Best on tap at the time of my visit.

The pub is open 12-15:00 all week then from 18-23:00 Monday to Saturday and 19:00-22:30 Sunday.

Telephone 01256 389777.

Walk No. 22

The pub is located on the B3046 in Preston Candover.

Approx distance of walk: 3 miles. Start at OS Map Ref SU 606418.

Parking is available in the car park directly opposite the village school.

From the days of William Cobbett's Rural Rides, the road through the picturesque Candover Valley has always provided a less direct but more notable route from Basingstoke to Winchester. Today the tiny Candover rivulet seldom rises beyond Brown Candover, the lowest of the three villages to which it gave its name. This doesn't seem to have troubled Preston Candover which though still small, is by far the largest with its shop, village hall and school. In ancient times Preston Candover was said to have had two wells, both of which were used by smugglers to hide their booty and one of which had an entrance large enough to contain a wag-gon and a team of horses. Quite where or how you'd hide a well with such an enor-mous entrance isn't recorded, but perhaps that particular legend is not entirely unrelated to another about the village of Stenbury (marked by Stenbury Drive in Preston Candover), which is said to have sunk beneath the earth somewhere around these parts!

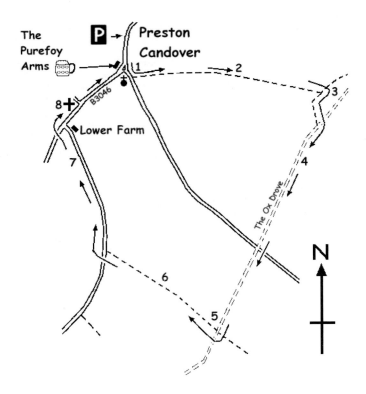

1. Start at the car park and walk to the green in the middle of the village opposite the Purefoy Arms. What must have been a one-duck pond on this green has long since disappeared, but the village's Victorian hand pump remains and continued to serve some households up until the 1950's. There doesn't seem to be a record of when it was installed, but it was probably around the same time as the lovely Victorian church of St Mary, high on the corner, which was designed by Sir Arthur Blomfield, one of the leading church architects of the era and built in 1884-5. Though as we shall see later this isn't the village's original Church, the large flat stone in the churchyard may signify that this site did hold some archaic pagan significance even before the new church was built or alternatively a small but unfulfilled rock garden. We take the road off to the left signposted towards Wield.

2. Our footpath lies between Church Farm Cottage with its old fire insurance mark and Church Farm, passing through a rather ornate iron gate and then down an avenue bordered by Ash trees. Shortly the path heads straight on out across a large field. At the top of this field the path passes through a gap in the hedge and continues straight on through the large field on the other side.

3. At the top of the field, after a short climb, we meet another gap through the hedge alongside a redundant stile. Pass through the gap then turn right to follow the hedgerow along the side of the field.

4. The field turns a corner by a small copse and as we go downhill, a track appears ahead just before we reach another copse on our left. Turn right and follow the track. This track, shown as The Ox Drove or Oxdrove on modern maps is also known as the Lun Way and is believed to date back to prehistoric times when it may have linked the hill forts at Woolbury Ring near Stockbridge, Oliver's Battery near Abbotstone Down and Ellisfield Camp nearer to Basingstoke. Over the years it was used as a salt road for bringing salt up from the south coast and also as one of the main drove roads linking downs at Abbotstone, Chilton and Preston with Ellisfield Common. The bewildering variety of shrubs and trees that line its route are happy testament to its venerable age.

5. Continue along the rolling track, with the nicely rippled hills of the Candover Valley opening out ahead. Cross straight on when you come to the road to Wield, then after ½

a mile or so look out for a signpost in a clearing on your left where a footpath cuts straight across the track. Here we turn right, off the track and through the hedge straight out across the field heading towards a double pole carrying a low voltage power line.

6. When you reach the foot of these poles, you'll see there is a gap in the hedge beneath. Go through the gap then turn right and follow the edge of this field.

7. This path leads us gradually downhill till we meet a road over a stile at the bottom. Turn right along the road, which leads us back towards Preston Candover, passing a lovely old barn with a built-in beehive at Lower Farm.

8. At the junction with the B3046, turn right again and continue along past a large brick building to a junction on the left. Turn down this road and you'll see that the building you've just passed is called the old vicarage. The reason for the vicarage lying so far from the current church lies just along the lane on the left, where a little metal gate brings you into the old cemetery with an ancient 12th century chancel, all that's left of the original church of St Mary's Preston Candover after the rest was destroyed in a disastrous fire in 1883. At least that's what one account says, another has it that the local clergy had spent so little on maintaining the place that by the 1850's it was little more than a ramshackle and dilapidated old barn with rotten furnishings and a graveyard so overcrowded that each time a new grave was dug, another long deceased ex-parishioner would be accidentally exhumed! What is certain is that much of the flint from the old church was wheeled down the road and used to help build the new, recycling having been invented in the building trade long before they'd even thought the planet might need saving. What they left behind is small, but nevertheless worthy of a good look round, there's a Saxon coffin lid that's been used as filler above the west door and two mass dials in the surround of the blocked up South door to begin with and it's well worth retrieving the key from one of the nearby keyholders listed for an inspection of the interior. Leaving the churchyard by the gate we came in by, return to the B3046 turning left at the road junction back to the middle of the village where the Purefoy Arms stands ready to quench your thirst.

The Coach and Horses, Rotherwick

Anyone who has experienced the hospitality and refreshment to found within the doors of this 16th-century inn would be left in no doubt about its capacity to tempt even the swiftest Coach and Horse to break its journey here. Not that many such equestrian conveyances pass by the doors on the way through Rotherwick these days, but regardless of vehicular contraption, once visited The Coach and Horses is a place you are certain to want to return to. This is a Hall and Woodhouse Inn, which is ably managed by Pat and Roger Ludlam and the standard of its ales can be judged by the blue Cask Marque plaque outside its door and its frequent inclusion in CAMRA's Good Pub Guide. The range of ales on offer is regularly revised but included at the time of my visit the Gribble Brewery's internationally challenging Plucking Pheasant, King and Barnes Sussex Ale and the old reliable Fursty Ferret.

The pub is open 11-15:00 and 17-23:00 Monday to Friday, 11-23:00 Saturday and 12-16:00 and 19-22:30 on Sunday. Food is available every lunchtime and evening.

Telephone 01256 762542

The pub is near the middle of the village along The Street.

Approx. distance of walk: 3 miles. Start at OS Map Ref SU 717565.

Parking is available along the verge of The Street, near the church and the pub.

Rotherwick seems such a lovely romantic name; it's hard to believe that it's derived from the Saxon phrase for cattle field. But don't let this put you off, Rotherwick's charms are many and today its cattle are few. This walk is quite easy and almost all on the level but make sure your footwear is suitable for the marshy bits around point 8.

1. Head down the main road from the pub and turn left into Wedmans Lane. Follow Wedmans lane till you reach a track billed as an "Unadopted Road" on your right. Follow this track round into Wedmans Place, then straight on along the grassy path to the right of the houses.

2. Pass through a kissing gate, straight across a gravel drive and through another kissing gate. Follow the right hand edge of this pasture to bring you round to yet a third kissing gate (popular here aren't they!). Passing through this, we cross over a lovely little wooden bridge and then proceed down a narrow path where overhanging branches may require the occasional stoop.

3. At the end of the footpath, we turn right along a made-up drive, straight across the road at the end and onto a gravel track signposted 'Footpath'. Ignore the metal gates where the track swings left; instead carry straight on towards the wood picking up a narrow but well used footpath, which swings to the right past a sign saying 'No Horses'.

4. The path becomes gravelled as we proceed; passing abandoned chicken arks and then some dilapidated farm buildings over on our right. At the end of this path we reach the main road, cross over and continue straight on to follow another rather more muddy path on the other side into the woodland.

5. Where you reach a junction in the path and the path straight ahead looks indistinct, we head off to the left along a more well-worn path, passing a large Rhododendron bush on our left and then shortly afterwards crossing a little concrete bridge with a metal handrail.

6. Presently our footpath emerges from the woods and we continue straight on along the right hand side of the next field. At the gap in the hedge on the right, we turn right, past a marker post and then keep right along the edge of this field.

7. As you approach the corner of the field you'll see a marker post on your right which points our way straight on and through the woods. At the end of this path we come to

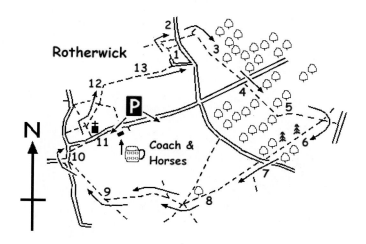

Walk No. 23

another road. Please take care here, as the view right isn't very good. Turn right along the road for a few yards before crossing over and entering the private car park 'For anglers only' at Rotherwick Lakes. Shortly you'll see a footpath sign on the right that points our way straight on along the edge of the wood.

8. The path gets very marshy at points along here and you may have to cut into the woods on your right to pass around them. Deer obviously aren't so fussy and one ambled straight across in front of me here just to prove it. Keep going straight on to pass through a gap and around a very derelict wooden gate, then along a thin grass strip between fields dodging round a large oak. Here a white cottage at Runten's Farm comes into view on the left as we head towards a metal kissing gate at the end of this section.

9. Go through the kissing gate then straight across a farm track into the field opposite following the well established path on the left hand side of the field. Carry straight on where the hedge ends, passing a couple of oaks on our right, a marker post and then to the left of what seems to be a wood consisting entirely of Rhododendrons. After this wood and just before you reach a lone tree, we turn sharp right across the open field heading towards a stile and some cottages at the top of the rise.

10. Crossing over the stile with its special little gate for dogs, we continue straight on across the next field. This brings us to another stile by a metal gate in the top corner, which we pass through to bring us to the road. Here we turn right, staying along the verge for a short distance till we meet a gravel bridleway on our right.

11. Turning down the bridleway we head towards the church, passing the duck pond complete with Mr and Mrs Ducks own little thatched nesting box and continuing on until we reach the road. Cross over and go through the gate to Rotherwick Church. As usual, the church rewards a closer inspection and among the points of note inside are the sketches of the church interior before its Victorian Revival and a very poetical inscription on the 17th century tomb of Ann Tylney on the chancel floor. Upon leaving the church, follow the gravel path around the church tower and look up to see the ancient graffiti scratched into the brickwork several feet up on the south side. The path continues straight on behind the church, past a bench to reach a metal kissing gate.

12. Passing through the gate, turn right along the edge of the field. Where you reach a point parallel with the end of the churchyard on your right, bear diagonally left across the field directly towards the large hedge beside Rooks Farm. The path runs alongside this hedge then crosses a farm track via two metal kissing gates into another field.

13. Continue straight across this field through another kissing gate to turn right along a little path skirting a barbed wire fence. Passing a rather insalubrious duck pond, continue into the next field straight on along a well-established footpath to the right of the hedge. At the end of this field is another kissing gate, passing through this we head straight across a small triangular field to another metal kissing gate in the corner. On the other side you find a gravel drive that leads you back onto the track we followed earlier, straight along to Wedmans Lane. At the Lane turn right and make your way back to the pub.

The Swan, Sherborne St John

A very popular pub with Basingstoke office staff for lunchtime and business meetings, the Swan is a managed house far removed from its origins as the village pub although it retains its original frontage and is still frequented by one or two locals who remember it 'in the old days'. The Swan is owned by the Laurel Pub Company and is currently managed by Heidi Wadsworth. It's divided broadly into two sections with one large area and a smaller cosy bit, which was the original bar. Three real ales are on tap, London Pride, Ringwood Bitter and Flowers Original, there are separate lunch and evening menus and a limited number of daily blackboard specials and they promise the fastest lunches in town! Open Baguettes and Wraps are also available at lunchtime.

The Swan is open 11-23:00 Mondays to Saturdays 12-22:30 Sundays.
Telephone 01256 850165

Approx. distance of walk: 5 miles. Start at OS Map Ref SU 623553

Parking is available in the village hall car park directly opposite the Swan or in the Swan car park providing you are using its facilities.

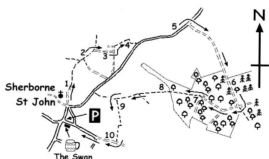

Sherborne is an old name for a clear stream and in this case that stream is the Wey Brook, a very minor tributary of the River Loddon, which we shall be passing over on our walk. The brook gave rise to two settlements, Monk or West Sherborne, which you can explore on one of the other walks in this book and Sherborne St John, which was established on lands once owned by a chap called Robert de Sancto Johanne. Several sections on this walk didn't appear to have seen visitors for a considerable time prior to my walk and you may find a stick handy to combat large nettles. Also please pay particularly close attention to the instructions at points 6 and 7, as these woodland paths have no marker arrows to help guide the way.

81

Walk No. 24

1. From the Swan, turn right along the road signposted towards Bramley. Where this road turns sharp right, we continue straight on along the drive towards Manor House Farm. You can take a short diversion to the church here on the left, although sadly it's generally locked shut and most of its attractions lay within. Continuing along the drive, we pass between the large cart shed and farm buildings (now converted into houses) before going through a small wooden gate alongside a large one and onto a grassy track.

2. Keep straight on along the track until you reach a stretch of wooden planking with a metal handrail where we cross the Wey Brook. At the end of the planking we cross a wooden stile out into an open field. Here we head diagonally to the right passing over the brow of the hill ahead then continuing in the same direction towards a large metal gate in the bottom corner. Cross the wooden stile beside this gate then turn right up the gravel track.

3. Shortly, up this small hill we have to climb over a metal gate (there's no stile and the gates locked shut), continuing to the top of the hill where we turn left along a concrete track.

4. A few yards along the track, we climb over the second of two metal gates. The derelict stile between being completely unusable. Then turning right, walk down the field along the left side of the hedgerow past some old and abandoned beehives. At the bottom of this field, turn right through the gap in the hedge beneath the twin poles carrying low voltage power cables, then along the hedge on the left until you reach a stile.

5. Cross the stile and follow the narrow path between the hedges turning right at the end over a wooden plank then through an old metal kissing gate under a large oak. This brings us out onto Vyne Road where we turn left along the road for about ½ mile. Turn right when you reach the gravel drive to Swingate Hill Cottages, and at the end of the drive continue straight on around the barrier and onto the track beyond.

6. We now proceed along a windy grassy track known as Marl's Lane. After running alongside fields, we enter a section where the woodland is dense on both sides and where parts of the track were wet and muddy despite a long dry spell. Here we pass a large rectangular metal tank off the track on the left and then reach a clear track directly across our path – the track ahead continues, but is suddenly reduced to a narrow footpath. Here we turn right along the clear track, which snakes left then right passing a large wooden post on the right.

7. Shortly, you reach a Y-shaped fork where you need to follow the right fork. There are more muddy bits along this stretch, but they are easy to pass around. After a fairly straight clear section, we come to a more indistinct part where at a point marked by a small wooden post off the path in the trees on the left, our path ahead bears slightly to the right and becomes vague as it is crossed at right angles by another equally vague path. Continue straight on over this 'crossroads' passing a large puddle at the side of the path after a few yards before coming onto a much clearer dirt path after crossing over a shallow dry ditch.

8. Follow the dirt path to emerge from the wood through a gap in the hedge onto a large open field. Here the public footpath had disappeared beneath a fully-grown crop but the route wasn't difficult to establish. Directly ahead on the face of the hill in front of us you can see a track running towards us just to the right of hedge following the same line. We head towards the foot of this track beneath and just to the right of a single pole supporting a low voltage power cable and left of a double pole supporting a different low voltage cable. We cross a wooden stile shortly after passing the brow of the hill continuing straight on over the next field down towards the opening that leads to the track.

9. We now cross a stile just to the left of the track and then follow the fence on the right up to the top of the field. At the top of the field don't pass through the squeezer stile ahead, instead turn left following a path along the top of the field. Continuing on in the next field after the path snakes right then left.

10. Pass through a narrow gap in the hedge at the bottom of this field, over a little wooden bridge and turn right along the gravel track. Keep straight on at the tarmac road junction to return to the Swan.

The White Hart, Sherfield on Loddon

A major coaching inn when it was built way back in the 17th Century, Sherfield's White Hart enjoys a slightly more relaxed position now that its particular end of the Reading Road has been transformed into a cul-de-sac. Far from deterring the wary traveller however, this detachment has actually made parking a lot easier and regulars now come from far and wide to enjoy the Sunday Roast, Steak and Ale Pie or more sophisticated epicurean house specialities such as ham rolled asparagus with cheddar cheese sauce. This is a free house run to exacting standards by Landlord Adrian Fyfe and his team and alongside the attractively decorated main bar, a comfortably furnished restaurant area displays a bewildering variety of miniature spirits gathered from around the globe. A wide selection of real ales are on offer to tempt amongst them Gales H.S.B and Pompey Premier.

The White Hart is open 11-14:30 and 17-23:00 Monday to Friday 11-23:00 Saturday and 12-22:30 Sunday.

There is a children's room and a garden, but dogs are not allowed in the pub. Telephone 01256 882280.

The pub is situated on the Reading Road in Sherfield on Loddon, just North of the Bramley crossroads.

Wyevale Country Gardens, Sherfield on Loddon

This large, modern garden centre stands opposite The Loddon School and as well as proffering a bewildering array of flowerage and horticulture and the concomitant apparatus, equipment and paraphernalia for the doing thereof, offers by way of its sunny little coffee shop the all too rare alternative of a restorative non-alcoholic beverage out in the countryside for those of us of an ambulatory disposition along with the usual range of basic snacks such as sandwiches, cakes and jacket potatoes.

The garden centre is open 09-18:00 Monday to Saturday and 10-16:30 Sunday. The coffee shop closes at 17:00 Monday to Saturday and 15:30 Sundays.

Telephone 01256 882239

Walk No. 25

Approx. distance of walk: 8 miles. Start at OS Map Ref SU 680580

Parking is available at the recreation ground on the corner of Reading Road and Bramley Road and also along Reading Road in Sherfield on Loddon. Alternatively you could park at the Garden Centre and start the walk at point 14

Mystery surrounds the change of name from Sherfield upon Loddon to Sherfield on Loddon that took place on O.S. maps in the 1960's. Perhaps the land sank because of wear and tear from the traffic along the A33? Today the A33 has been diverted around the village, but speeding traffic along the Reading Road has been substituted by a veritable plague of signposts and traffic markers instead! Hopefully someone will tidy this up one day and raise Sherfield well and truly back up upon the Loddon, and perhaps regain a few more of the 'Best Kept Village' prizes it captured a few years ago. Certainly nothing should deter you from sampling the village delights and this long but fairly easy-going walk around some of the beautiful countryside that surrounds it. The path is a little vague in parts, but follow the map and instructions closely and you won't have any difficulties.

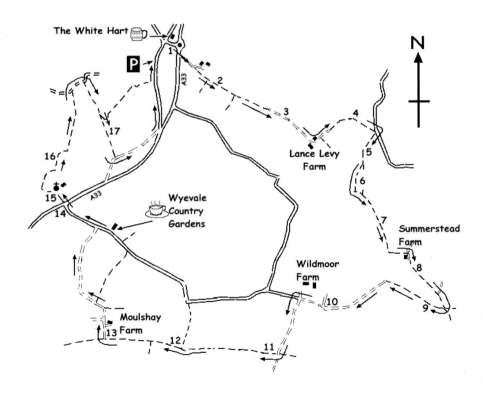

1. Starting at the village Post Office, proceed along Breach Lane and take the footpath into the trees directly past the front of Breach Lane Chapel. Follow it left at the end and carefully cross the A33.

2. On the opposite side, follow the signposted footpath more or less straight on down a gravel track. Just past the houses, cross the flattened fence on your right and continue straight on over the field parallel to the route of the track. The old barn we see over to the left was built over 600 years ago and is one of the oldest buildings in the village. Continuing to the left of Laundry Copse – a name derived from the period when Sherfield's lord of the manor was responsible for keeping order amongst the Kings laundresses, we shortly pass a rather disgruntled looking farm trailer on our right and a large oak on our left along a mud track and then along the right hand edge of the next field.

3. At the end we cross a small footbridge and pass through a hedge to emerge in what is now Sherfield Oaks Golf Course. Keep to the gravel track straight on past the golf course buildings and then along a mud track to the right of a line of old oaks, ducking if you should hear anyone shout 'fore'. In a little while we reach Lance Levy farm where we turn left just past the brick cottages and down a lovely grassy lane.

4. Passing through a gate at the foot of the short hill, go straight on across the field ahead (skirting round a fallen tree which was there at the time of writing) towards the gap on the opposite side which you'll find is a small bridge over one of the many brooks and streams that make up the Loddon at this point. Cross the bridge then follow the well-trodden path diagonally right over the next field aiming to the right of an electricity pylon, turning right where you meet the stream again and then straight on towards a metal gate.

5. At the gate, we turn 90° to the right to head back at right angles to the direction of our approach over the same field towards a wooden stile, which becomes more obvious as you walk towards it! Cross the stile and the path continues in a straight line ahead clipping the hedge on the right and then running roughly parallel with the bank of the stream.

6. When you reach a barbed wire fence with a footbridge amongst trees to the right, go left around the end of the fence and then forward alongside the bank of the stream. We then cross another stile, before turning left across a narrow footbridge and then along the path right. (Not straight on across the second footbridge.) We meet another watercourse shortly from the left and pass through a neatly sliced gap in the massive remains of a fallen tree.

7. After crossing a second fallen tree via a neatly cut step, we cross another small wooden bridge. On the other side follow the narrow well-trodden path across the field roughly in the direction of Summerstead Farm ahead. Where you near the hedge, ignore the stile on the left but carry straight on parallel to the hedge, over a concrete pipe and then turn left at the end of the hedge. Follow the path straight on through the gate in the wooden fence leading between farm buildings and turns right along the gravel track in front of the farm house.

8. Pass through the wooden gate on the left just after the house and turn right along a very narrow field bounded either side by hedgerows. Carry straight on past the wooden post at the far end following the left hand edge of the field to a metal kissing gate.

9. We now pass through a wood for a short distance before coming to a junction with other paths at an HCC marker post where we turn right. This brings us to a stile, cross the stile and turn right following the path along the right hand edge of the field.

10. Pass through the gap at the end of the field and over a concrete bridge. Then continue straight along the right hand edge of the next field, through a metal gate and straight on along a mud track. Shortly the track becomes concrete and we cross an open-sided bridge over the Loddon. Just after the bridge, we turn left off the track over a small wooden footbridge marked with a yellow HCC arrow then sharp right along a narrow path through a dell.

11. We emerge on the corner of a tarmac road where we turn sharp left passing through the gate marked 'Long Copse Cottage'. After about ½ mile where this track twists to the right, you'll find a stile next to a metal gate on the right, which is our next path. Passing over the stile we go right along the edge of the field passing an old Hawthorn next to a stump and then a line of five young oaks. At the top of the field cross the stile by the metal gate continuing straight on along the left edge of the next field then over another stile.

12. Continuing straight on, skirting the woods on our right, we pass through another

gap in the woods into another field. A short distance along you'll find a stile on the right which we cross into the wood. At the fork in the path, turn left and follow a beautiful long straight wooded path.

13. At the far end we meet with another clear path by an HCC marker post and here we turn right, carrying straight on where we meet a gravelled farm track, passing to the left of Moulshay Farm and ignoring the track of to the left a short time after. Continue along this main track until you reach a minor road, the garden centre is 100 yards along to your right.

14. Leaving the garden centre, turn right along the minor road, we pass a Victorian Post-box unusually set into the wall of 'The Old Forge' on the left before reaching the junction with the A33. Cross with great care and a little patience and proceed up the gravelled drive of Sherfield Court between the brick pillars towards St Leonard's Church.

15. Sadly the church is not open for the occasional visitor, but you can ponder over the simple grave of John Silver just on the right as you enter the churchyard. After 250 years the stone is now a little difficult to read, but the skull and crossbones are still very clear. Shiver me timbers, could this really be Long John? Our path passes the main entrance to the church on the right and the rather unusual Victorian family tomb of the illustrious Pigotts Stainsby Conants on the left – including that of Francis Stainsby Conant Pigott, former MP for Reading and one-time Governor of the Isle of Man.

16. Leaving the churchyard by the stile on the far side, turn right along the top edge of the field where we skirt a high bank, which surrounds a medieval water-filled moat. Its rare survival mainly due to its adoption as an ornamental boating pond when nearby Sherfield Court was built in the Georgian era. Although invisible to the walker, the popularity of the moat with wildlife can be judged by the large number of Canada Geese resting in the field alongside while I passed. Our walk now runs parallel to a line of Poplars planted in the 1920's then turns right at the bottom of the field to run through Gulley Copse and then left along the hedge up the next field.

17. Crossing an unusual metal stile at the top of the field, continue along the dirt track on the left side of the next field then over a wooden stile at the far end. Turn right along the road for a 100 yards then right at the

signposted footpath. Follow this path down the left hand field edge, through the gap by Katy's Copse and continuing straight on down the next field. At the bottom we meet the tarmac of a twisty former section of A33 bypassed in 1968, turn left here and follow the old road which will lead you directly to Reading Road and back to the village.

The Red Lion, Mortimer West End

Surrounded on three sides by, and just a stones-throw away from the Hampshire Berkshire border, Mortimer West End - as you may have gathered from its title is a small hamlet just to the west of it's larger Berkshire namesake. Quite why the border so studiously avoids this portion of the lands owned at the time of the doomsday book by a chap called Ralf Mortimer isn't clear, but the settlement evolved on the corner of Aldermaston Heath just up the hill from a popular ford across the West End Brook and where the Red Lion began its life as a farmhouse. A detailed history of the building and many old photographs of the area adorn the walls of this attractive timber-beamed inn where what appear to be detached buildings outside blend seamlessly within to provide large separate dining areas.

Owned by Hall and Woodhouse, the pub has a lot of character and according to Landlady Jo Oakley may play host to a ghostly female with long black curly hair. Though none of the staff would admit to seeing her, there was a general acknowledgement that a mysterious female voice would occasionally be heard when the pub was at its quietist. Not that this is a regular occurrence though, as the pub is extremely popular throughout the day drawing in many Silchester visitors for its tasty, largely homemade food. There is a large garden and play area and pets are welcome in designated areas.

The pub is open 11-23:00 Monday to Saturday and 12-22:30 Sunday with food available 12-14:30 and 19-21:30 Monday to Saturday and up to 21:00 Sunday. Telephone 0118 9700169

Walk No. 26

The pub is situated along Church Road north of Calleva Roman Town.

Approx. distance of walk: 6 miles. Start at OS Map Ref SU 635636

There is parking for 3 or 4 cars opposite the chapel just up the hill from the pub or you can park in the large car park just outside the roman town and start the walk at Point 2. Tall nettles and a very narrow path at section 8 could make this walk uncomfortable for anyone in short trousers and a stick could be handy.

The mighty Roman walls of Calleva Atrebatvm have stood up well to the ravages of time but even their mighty strength could not protect the town within from the neglect of humanity. Cast aside like a redundant carrier bag 1500 years ago, the town fell into ruin and eventually disappeared beneath the soil. About 1000 years later, people began to get curious about the bumps in the meadow and since then the town has enjoyed a bit of a renaissance. OK, so at the moment the vast level fields within the walls looks just about as glamorous as any other field you've ever come across, but just imagine, in 1500 years time this could be just how your ancestors will see Basingstoke! Pay particular attention as to which gate to go through at point 3 as there are several to choose from and the route is not as obvious as it appears on the OS map.

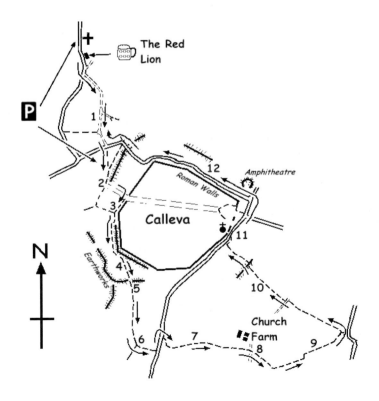

1. Walk down the hill past the Red Lion. Ignore the first track on the left immediately after the pub and take the second a short distance further on signposted 'Right of Way'. Large people should observe the notice and keep to the centre of the track. The track leads us up Stone Hill, bringing us out onto a narrow road opposite the main car park for the Roman Town.

2. Go straight across into the car park heading for the three tall information pillars. Go right just beyond them and follow the path that runs alongside one of the outer earthworks. Built before the stone walls to protect the town, these banks were originally 30ft high or more. Follow the gravel track till it passes through the wall and then turn right.

3. Here the track bears sharp right to a stile; a second path appears to lead straight on and a third through a kissing gate almost straight on. We take a less obvious path to the right of this through another kissing gate marked on the gatepost with a white arrow just to the right of a large metal gate, which will take you into a field. Keep to the left hand side of this field where we shortly rejoin the cities outer earthwork.

4. At the corner of the field, follow the yellow marker arrow along a short track through a kissing gate into the next field. Here we head diagonally to the right following the direction of the yellow arrow towards another kissing gate you can see over on the far side of the field.

5. Once over the kissing gate we cross another ancient earthwork, also part of the original fortifications for Calleva and thought by some to have been built upon even older defences established by the Belgic tribes who first settled here, only later to find themselves allied with the invading Romans. Fortunately these days we only have to battle against the undergrowth through this section to take us to another stile.

6. Cross this stile and go straight on over the next field passing just to the left of the dense woodland you see ahead. Keep to the side of these woodlands till they end abruptly just past a long dead tree stump. Our path continues straight ahead over the field along a slight ridge, passing between two large fallen trees. Beyond these there is a three-fingered signpost where we continue left now along the edge of the field. Follow this edge of the field round the corner to a stile by a metal gate.

7. Over the stile, go right along the minor road and very shortly you'll come to another footpath signposted on the right. Over the stile, keep to the right hand edge of the field with the red brick Church Lane Farm very dominant ahead. The next stile takes us slightly to the left, but once across return to follow the right hand side of the field.

8. The next stile takes you out of the field and along a very narrow path between wire fences, then over another stile onto a wider track past the farm. Two more stiles take us over a tarmac farm road, and then keeping to the right through a very small field yet another stile to a much larger field.

9. We follow the right hand edge of this field for a short while before crossing diagonally to the left towards a wooden stile marked with white paint on either side. Cross the stile and follow the right hand edge of the next field until it turns sharp right where we again head diagonally – this time to the right to pick up the hedge again over on the far side. Here a short diversion to the right brings you to an interesting meadow, which thanks to the Countryside Commission you are free to explore. It contains a 13th Century moat and fishponds and hundreds of lovely willow trees planted for the manufacture of cricket bats. Returning to our original path along the edge of the field, cross the stile in the far corner by a big oak into another small field.

10. Here we again stick to the right hand edge of the field, past a stile and then following around the corner where the field turns sharp left. At the top of the field we cross another stile onto a track and here we turn left for a few yards then right to follow a grassy path alongside rather stagnant looking small ponds with a sign advising 'Conservation Area – Keep all dogs on leads'. Continue along till you reach the top where we cut through the hedge by a wooden shooting platform over a ditch and into the next field – a white arrow on a tree does mark this route, but is very difficult to spot. The hedgerow marks the line of another outer fortification for Calleva while the small squat church of St Mary's atop the hill ahead marks the line of the Roman Walls.

11. Follow the left hand hedge through the next field, and around its turns alongside the road until you come to the gap directly opposite the church. Go straight across and into the churchyard and if you've time have a good look round. I thought one of the nicest features was the simple little fish weathervane up on the roof, but amongst

other things you'll find outside is the tomb of General Sir Edmund Haythorne KGB who, during a long and illustrious career served both in the Crimea and at the siege of Sebastopol. Inside you'll find a very comprehensive guidebook to all the glories of St Mary's, so I'll leave you in its capable hands to ogle sagaciously at the ogee-headed tomb recess with its uncommonly big cusps.

12. Exit the churchyard and return to the road, turn left, continuing straight on past the junction on your right and then turning left onto Wall Lane at the next junction. Follow Wall Lane for ½ mile and it will bring you back to the car park we met at point 2. Return to the pub along the track down Stone Hill.

Roman Wall, Silchester

Silchester Church

The Bull Inn, Stanford Dingley

For the better part of 600 years, The Bull Inn has sat almost directly opposite the small village green in Stanford Dingley, quietly watching the ebb and flow of the seasons and the little changed scenes of everyday village life. Today this venerable freehouse is run as a happy four-way partnership between Kate and Robert Archard and Carol and Robin Walker and is renown in the district for its extensive and ever-changing menu. I called in on a Monday, which happened to be Oriental Night, and amongst the evenings Eastern delicacies were Thai Red Fish Curry, Thai Beef Salad or Szechwan Spicy Chicken. Such exotica is not restricted to such weekly events though, the days specials on the blackboard listed delights such as Marinated Wild Boar Belly with Grain Mustard Dressing or Seared Sea Bass Fillet with Pea Mash, Lime Butter and Vegetable Sauce and a dozen other equally colourful delights to tempt the pallet, all at very reasonable prices.

The Bull is open 11-15:00 and 18-23:00 Monday to Saturday and 12-15:00 and 19-22:30 on Sundays with food available 12-14:30 Monday to Sunday and 18:30-21:30 Monday to Saturday 19-21:00 Sunday. Children and dogs are welcome in designated areas.

Telephone 01189 744409

Walk No. 27

Approx. distance of walk: 5 miles. Start at OS Map Ref SU 575717.

Limited parking is available on the verge next to the church or - providing you obtain prior permission from the landlord - in the car park of The Bull Inn.

As far as I know to date, a standard reference work has yet to be produced that concentrates on such beautifully graphic English names as nutty-slack or Mangle-wurzel. But if such a work did exist then I'm sure its pages would bear prominently Stanford Dingley with its hint at fairy-toed wading and its stockier, broad-shouldered neighbour Tutts Clump. Evocative place-names aside, the hills and vales of the (oriental?) Pang Valley hold many delights and I hope this little walk will serve as a polite introduction to further explorations of the region.

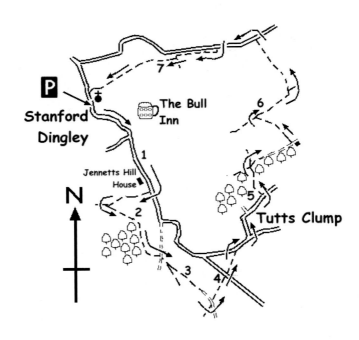

1. From the church, turn left along the road and through the village. Along the way we pass the Bull Inn and carry straight on up the hill at the junction. We pass Jennetts Hill House and the old village pump before taking the footpath indicated off to the right.

2. We pass through a kissing gate and into a field where we continue along the right hand hedgerow. Three-quarters of the way across the field we come to a fingerpost where we turn almost back on ourselves 40º to the left to take another path diagonally back across the field towards a marker post you can see at the top situated between the dense copse to the right and a group of 4 or 5 small bushes on the left. Pause at the top of the field to take in the view back and then continue uphill along the edge of the copse to a stile just around the corner.

3. Over the stile, we then climb a steep narrow path through the copse to reach another stile at the top of the hill where we enter a field. We follow the right edge of this field, to exit by another stile on the far side. Here we pass along a woodland path continuing straight across a gravel road onto the byway opposite. Shortly, where the path splits follow the narrow path to the left indicated by a marker post and keep left at the next fork. Before very long we reach another marker post opposite a house called Gorselands where we continue straight on onto a gravel drive.

4. Continue on to the next marker post just after a garage and before a panel fence where we turn left along a fenced path that brings us out onto the road alongside Glenvale Nurseries. Go straight over the road and through the kissing gate opposite and follow a path straight on across this field exiting through another kissing gate on the far side.

5. This brings us out onto Cock Lane where we turn right and then turn left just past the reservoir towards Tutts Clump. Continue along past the beautiful Edwardian houses in this hamlet to a narrow path on the left just past two of the largest houses Kimber and Woodhurst. This path takes us down a fairly steep descent through woodlands to a junction with another path half way down the hill from which point there are good views across the Pang valley over to the row of hills 2-3 miles away on the other side.

6. Turn right along the path, which widens into an old track through woodlands until you reach the cottages at the end. Turn left here over a stile and along a grassy path through two sets of tall gates to meet another path after the second gate. Here turn right continuing straight along the gravel bridleway at the end of the path. Turn left at the wooden gate to pass through a metal gate and onto a beautiful waterside path, continue straight on, on the little gravel path after the bridge.

7. Turn left when you reach the road and then left at the next footpath sign which takes you into a field and then along to the right alongside the hedgerow. You pass through two gates over a drive and then turn left at the corner of the field to another gate shortly on the right. Through the gate we cross a narrow field and exit over a stile into another field, here we follow the right hand field boundary to a point where the hedgerow turns right where our path heads diagonally left across the field directly towards the church steeple. We exit the field through a metal gate, continuing towards the church across the next field, passing through a wooden kissing gate then along the left hand edge of the field to exit by another kissing gate into the churchyard.

The Plough Inn, Little London

The tiny nooks and snug corners you'll find within the little Plough Inn give it a wonderfully comfy atmosphere and belie its mere 350-year existence. Here is a pub that feels much older than that and certainly one that must have changed little since it was first established – at the time well within the bounds of nearby Pamber Forest. Landlord Terry Brown clearly enjoys running this wonderful Free House tucked away in the hamlet of Little London and although food is limited to a range of baguettes during lunch and evening, this is compensated for by a comparatively wide range of real ales given the pubs small size with an ever-changing line-up of guests. On tap at the time of my visit were Ringwood and Adnams Best alongside the delicious Otter Bright and that was despite the cellar temporarily out of action due to building work. There is a small garden at the back; children are welcome along with dogs on a lead.

Opening hours are 12-14:30 Monday to Friday 12-15:00 weekends and in the evenings 18-23:00 Monday to Saturday and 19-22:30 Sunday.

Telephone 01256 850628.

The pub is on the Silchester Road in Little London

Approx. distance of walk: 6 miles. Start at OS Map Ref SU 623593.

Limited parking is available in a lay-by almost directly opposite St Stephens Hall in Little London, alternatively find a spot in Tadley Hill and begin the walk at point 9.

If Basingstoke saw expansion in the 1960's then Tadley positively exploded, with a warren-like medley of houses and tracks branching far and wide from its diminutive roots and today in parts it more closely resembles the housing pattern you'll find in the Mediterranean than a small British town. This walk glances the town at its southern end, where most of older buildings and its origins lie and takes in its original tiny church and a very small part of one of its greatest assets - Pamber Forest - along the route.

1. From St Stephens Hall, turn right up the hill into the middle of Little London. Passing a rather cosy little bus shelter just outside the kennels, continue till you reach a beautiful ornamental fir tree in the garden of Wychwood. Here we turn up the gravel drive directly opposite just next to the 'single file traffic' sign following a footpath sign that is shrouded in foliage. Continue straight to the top and underneath a one-bar gate to follow a path along the left hand edge of this field for a short distance and then pass over a stile on your left.

2. Go straight down the field and over the stile you can see in the middle at the bottom. Keep straight on across the next enclosure then over another stile along a narrow path keeping to the barbed wire fence on the left. Leave this field by another stile to bring you to a tarmac road.

3. Turn right along the road and keep going till you reach a group of houses on your right. We take the path indicated by the footpath sign on the left just opposite a house called Lynton. The path crosses a stile alongside an old tin shed, down the left hand side

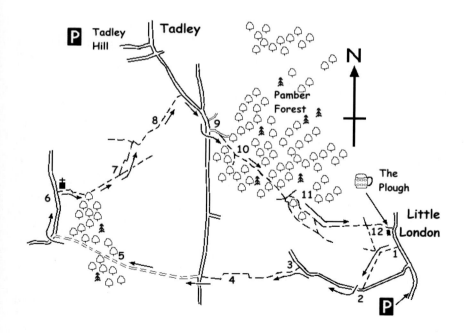

95

of a small enclosure to a small bridge. Make your way past the movable wooden poles and over the fence at the far end then, crossing another small enclosure clamber through the unorthodox permanent hole in the fence opposite out into a large field beyond.

4. Turn right and our footpath follows the hedgerow around this field, even where it turns sharp right (where like me you might come face to face with a large deer lurking just around the corner) and then sharp left at the other end. After a little straight bit, it's left then right again as we pass Wigmore Farm on our left and the Nursery on our right. We exit the field over a stile in the corner, which brings us onto the A340.

5. Carefully make your way straight across the A340 to pickup a footpath along a farm track directly opposite. Keep straight on where track crosses the middle of an open field and plunges into a wood – through the wood several tracks lead off our main one but there are plenty of signs to keep you on course leading us out the other side to a point where we eventually meet a minor road.

6. Turn right along the road and shortly we approach one of Tadley's hidden gems, the delightful little church of St Peter. Our path actually lies to the right just before the church, but a quick tour around the outside of this lovely little building will add much to your day out. The brick tower is the oldest part and high up you can see the builder's mark RH 1680. Also, if you're like me you'll ponder over the significance of the unusual heart shaped embellishment above the north door on the far side. Having pondered, return to the path we came to before the church, follow along the left hand hedgerow of the field as it curves around to the right continuing straight on where we reach the corner and the path cuts into the wood. Ignore the track to the left and right and keep straight on along a narrow path, through a clearing and then out of the wood over a stile.

7. The path continues straight on cutting diagonally across this field towards some large trees on the opposite side where you'll find a stile alongside a large metal gate. Do not cross the stile, instead turn left and continue along the right hand hedgerow to cross into the next field by another stile in the top corner. Continue along the right hand hedge then follow the marker post straight on across a wooded ditch and around the side of a metal fence that appears to block the way.

8. Past the metal fence, as you'll see our path turns sharp right following a narrow gap between a fence on the left and the hedgerow on the right. The path turns left at the corner of the field, shortly crossing a stile into a more wooded section at the end of which we cross a small bridge then climb up a bank straight into a grassy field. Follow the well-trodden route straight up the hill then over to the left where a very nice new wooden stile takes you onto a gravel drive. Turn right along the drive to return to the A340 we crossed earlier.

9. Turn right along the footpath and cross where it's safe to do so to pass the Fighting Cocks. Here you can stop and partake of a little refreshment if you wish or continue along the verge alongside the A340 to the second metal footpath sign, just before the large road sign informing you that you've reached Pamber Green.

10. The path takes us down a gravel track, after the small brick building passing through a gap in the fence on the left of to continue along the track. Just after this we reach a small clearing where we turn off the main track down a clear path to the right. Shortly, after passing a prominent oak tree on the right, we reach a clear fork in the path where we turn left.

11. Continue along this path ignoring minor paths off to either side, we pass through a long narrow clearing into a more wooded section to reach a clear junction, here our path – the main one - turns sharp left, a narrow path joins from the right and another path jinks round a tree ahead to continue more or less straight on. We continue round to the left where a short distance further on you'll see a large earth bank on the left, where we take the path off to the right.

12. Ignore minor paths off on either side as our path winds along and after weaving right then left, running roughly parallel with fields to the right, we reach the end of our path with an open field ahead barred by a one bar gate. Go around or under the gate as you see fit and follow the well-trodden path straight on across the middle of the field (another well-trodden path here went right to join the footpath along the right-hand hedgerow although this doesn't appear on the OS map) across the field. Over the brow of the hill the path heads toward a small wooden gate, we don't go through the gate, but pass to the right with the hedge to our left exiting the field by a narrow path to emerge just outside the Plough.

The Hoddington Arms, Upton Grey

According to current landlords David and Monica McCutcheon, the 300-year-old Hoddington Arms in Upton Grey began life as three small cottages, which have been slowly augmented and elaborated down the years to evolve into the spacious, welcoming pub we find today. This Greene King House is divided into two main areas with the main bar separate from the restaurant. There is also a very large garden to the rear with a patio and children's play area.

The home-cooked-menu is wide ranging with something to interest all-comers from traditional Steak and Chips or a generous Cheddar Ploughman's to rather more exotic delights such as Swordfish with a Caper and Sun dried Tomato Crust or Honey-glazed Breast of Duck on a bed of noodles. To wash down such delightful delectations IPA, Old Speckled Hen and Ruddles are the resident ales and David is hoping to introduce various guest ales in the not to distant future.

The pub is open 12-15:00 and 18-23:00 Monday to Saturday and to 22:30 Sundays, Food is available 12-14:00 and 19-21:00 all week except Sunday evenings.

Telephone 01256 862371

Walk No. 29

The pub is situated along Bidden Road which is the main road through Upton Grey.

Approx. distance of walk: 7 miles. Start at OS Map Ref SU 700483

Parking is available in the recreation ground car park at the end of Little Hoddington Close or - providing you obtain prior permission from the landlord - in the car park of The Hoddington Arms.

Few villages can rival Upton Grey for its picturesque charm, from its marvellous duck pond to its magnificent church, it is the embodiment of an idyllic country village and a deserved multiple winner of Hampshire's best kept village competition. Despite some recent growth, it remains remarkably untouched by the twin traumas of road transport and over-engorged housing developments and long may it remain so. I'm pleased to report that the roads in the area have however seen considerable improvement since the 18th century when the official route between Basingstoke and Upton Grey was reportedly in such a wretched state that traffic was forced to divert south through Hackwood Park to obtain clear passage.

This is a relatively straightforward walk, but a walking stick may prove beneficial in dealing with the overgrown paths south of Weston Patrick (point 7) and around Hoddington Farm (point 8) and a compass for crossing the field you meet at point 8 where signposts had unfortunately been removed and there are no natural reference points to navigate by.

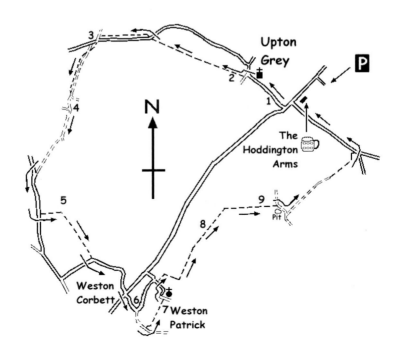

1. From the Hoddington Arms, turn right at the village pond along the road signposted to Tunworth, there is a great deal to admire along here from the decorative tiling on the walls of Spinners, to the splendid little door on Vicarage Cottage. The church is generally locked, but its still worth exploring the churchyard where I particularly enjoyed the epitaph on one tomb - 'Lord I commit my soul to thee, accept my sacred trust, receive the nobler part of me and watch my sacred dust' - quite a jolly ring to it! Leaving the churchyard, continue on up the hill.

2. On the corner by the grand metal gates, follow the footpath sign along the tarmac track on the left, turning right soon after along another signposted footpath up the right hand side of the field. We pass through a narrow copse on the way continuing past this into the next field. We exit at the corner by a signpost onto a road where we cross straight over, through a narrow gap in the hedge on the other side to turn left along a permissive path around the edge of this field.

3. The buildings of Basingstoke come into view over the hills to the right along the way, then we leave this field over a grassy bank at the bottom corner and onto the gravel track beyond where we turn left back to the road. Again cross straight over and onto a footpath on the other side. The path passes through a small wood then straight over a tarmac drive and along the left hand hedgerow of the field on the opposite side – with a lovely little footpath sign to confirm the route. Some of the once pollarded trees along here would fare very well in a knobbly knees competition.

4. At the end of the field, continue straight on where the path turns onto a track and ignore the turning shortly to the left. Also where the grey gravel turns right and gives way to concrete, continue straight on along the edge of the field onto brown gravel. Ignore the track shortly off to the left into a field, keeping right to eventually exit from the track through a gate onto a tarmac road at the far end.

5. Turn left along the road for a short distance and then left over a stile just beyond Reed Farm House. There is a glorious view from here down the hill to the old barn at Manor Farm in Weston Corbett. Follow the track ignoring the stiles into the garden on your left, turn right just in front of the old farm buildings down a grass track exiting through a gap at the end then straight down across the field directly towards a red roofed

house at the bottom. The path running parallel to a line of low voltage power lines just to the left. We exit this field at the bottom via a grassy track to the left of the red-roofed house, over a stile and onto a road where we turn left.

6. Follow the road past the old farm house and farm buildings, straight over at the crossroads then where the little road turns left by a white metal fence, we take the track off to the right marked ' no vehicular right of way.' Follow this bridleway uphill for a short distance passing a small brick building in the field to the left, then at the top of that field we pass through a narrow gap – a squeezer stile without the squeeze – built into the fence on the left to follow a rather unkempt footpath along the left hand edge of the field.

7. Cross the stile to the left just past the tennis courts continuing straight on along the path to the left of a fence, we shortly cross another stile into a field and then another almost immediately back out of it onto a lane beside Manor Farm.

8. Turn left down the lane past the lovely little church of St Laurence to turn right shortly along a narrow path hidden just to the right of the gravel drive of the cottage on the corner. Cross over the stile at the to continue straight on up the hill in the field with the fence on your right. Passing the rather baronial Manor Farm building, turn left when you reach a point alongside the hedgerow half of the way up the field and turn left to pass alongside it with the hedgerow on your left. On the far side of the field exit via another stile and continue straight on across the next field, continuing past the point where hedgerow ends on your left to pass through a gap in the hedge on the far side.

9. From here the path lies almost directly east, crossing this field diagonally to the right to a track over on the far side. Follow the track into the wood past some old and very deep pits. On the other side of the woods, turn left at a marker post to follow a track along the left side of the field. At the end of this track we reach a metal gate. From here we go diagonally across the next field to the left, clipping the fence at the end of the brown metal buildings straight towards the house in the far corner. Once there you'll find a stile just to the left of the house. Cross the stile and work your way round to the road at the front, turn left and return to Upton Grey.

The Silk Mill Tearooms, Whitchurch

The ta-pocketa-pocketa-pocketa that accompanied Walter Mitty's dreamy adventures almost becomes reality at Whitchurch Silk Mill where the pleasing brick-faced exterior hides a large and undisguisedly industrial setting for its popular tearoom.

Only the fabulous, shimmering silks they produce here could engender such a sufficiently Mitty-like state in anyone for them to mistake this interior for a vision of loveliness, and as I sat watching contented visitors gossip happily over their refreshments, the far-off rhythmic accompaniment of the thrashing waterwheel deep in the bowels of the place made me wonder if it had indeed induced some Mitty-like spell, reminded as I was of that tea-party scene in Carry-on Up the Khyber.

Aesthetics aside, this is a fine place to take tea and architectural niceties are soon forgotten thanks to the excellence of the home-made food, steaming beverages and outstanding service. If I can mercilessly paraphrase that well-known proverb, you can't make an attractive Silk Mill tearoom out of the sow's ear that is a Georgian industrial interior!

Admission to the Silk Mills tearoom and souvenir shop is free, but there is a charge to tour the interior of the mill.

The Mill is open Tuesday to Sunday and Bank Holiday Mondays from 10:30-16:30.

Telephone 01256 892065

The Silk Mill is located in Winchester Street near the middle of Whitchurch.

Approx. distance of walk: 10 miles. Start at OS Map Ref SU 462481.

There are several free car parks in Whitchurch, all of which are located within a couple of minutes of the start of our walk but please check notices for restrictions. This walk loops around the town and there are numerous potential shortcuts you can take if the full walk is too much however do make sure not to miss the short section from the Fulling Mill along the Test to the church (Point 24), as this is one of the highlights of the village.

The white church that is believed to have given Whitchurch its name may have long disappeared, but today's lovely town has a plethora of visual attractions for us happy wanderers to enjoy. As some of the buildings may suggest, in the early 18th century a few of the towns inhabitants did rather well, chiefly through the industries of papermaking, silk manufacture and the production of woollen cloth and other textiles. Later during the coaching era Whitchurch became an important crossroads between Salisbury and Exeter in the West, Oxford and Newbury in the north, Basingstoke and London to the east and Winchester and Southampton to the south and this spawned the enormous White Hart Hotel. In its heyday Whitchurch returned two members of Parliament (despite a population of less than 2,000) and the now redundant town hall also reflects a more weighty influence in times gone by, however that was then, Whitchurch lost its parliamentary duo and status as a 'rotten borough' with the reform act in 1832, and a familiar bank logo long ago took the 'town' out of the hall. The Square is now a roundabout and bypassed and politically emasculated, Whitchurch has become a peaceful backwater ripe for us walkers to enjoy!

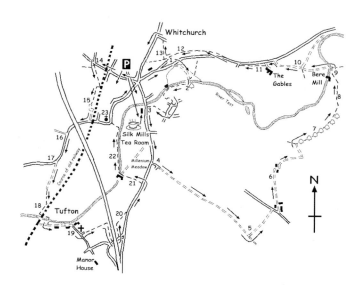

Walk No. 30

1. Start from the White Hart Hotel. Head east (away from the village centre) along London Street. Along the way, we pass the old Cinema on the right, and then just past the turning for the Lynch, the old County Police Station on the left. We turn right into Town Mill Lane just opposite Voters Cottage. This cottage owes its name to the pre-reform days of parliament when the Earl of Portsmouth bought it solely to qualify him for voting rights in the borough.

2. Along Town Mill Lane we cross a tiny branch of the Test where we can stop to admire a few of the large trout in its waters, before following this stream along the lane. Wild ducks patrol this area, so make sure you have enough bread to defend yourself. At the end of the lane, take the path straight ahead to cross the footbridge over the main course of the Test alongside Town Mill, one of two former corn mills in the town. Here the Trout seem to be about twice the size they were at the other bridge, so don't fall in. Continue over the bridge and then take the tarmac path to the right, past an enormous Beech tree.

3. The white building we pass on our right that precariously overhangs the river is known as Fisherman's Cottage and was used – appropriately enough - as a lodge for fishermen. At the end of this tarmac path, we reach a corner of McFauld Way. Carry straight on, crossing over Sheppard Close and following the grass verge towards the playground. Turn right where you reach the playground, along a short tarmac path then right and left down a narrow walled passageway to emerge on Winchester Road almost directly opposite the Silk Mill. This fine Georgian building built from chalk blocks faced with red brick features a prominent clock added in 1815 to commemorate the Battle of Waterloo. Ducks fly in from miles around to visit the pool by the bridge opposite and quack as small children throw food at them.

4. Turn left along Winchester road, which we now follow for about ½ of a mile, pausing briefly to enjoy the lovely fish gate to Millennium Meadow over on your right. Shortly after you've passed this, turn left along Webbs Farm Close.

5. Follow the well-defined footpath straight on at the end of the road, climbing up a shallow hill with hedgerows on both sides. At the top where we emerge from the hedgerows, continue straight on. There are good views either side back down the hill. After a short while, the main track turns left with another route continuing straight ahead, we follow the track round to the left towards the farm buildings.

6. When you come to the road turn right, then after 100 yards turn left to follow the concrete roadway between Southfield Farm buildings and down the hill. Go through the gate at the bottom of the hill and continue along the track around to the right of the barn.

7. Continue downhill into the Test valley and a little way further follow the track round sharply to the left till it meets an open field alongside a redundant stile. Turn right here and follow the path along the top edge of this pasture beneath the trees of Coombedown Hanger.

8. Towards the end of the Hanger where the field begins to open out, cross the field diagonally to the left and head for the distant stile ahead.

9. Cross the stile and follow the path alongside the capped wall, and you'll emerge to the right of Bere Mill with a good view of the old bridge. Bere Mill started life as a corn mill and the sign on it that you might just be able to make out states 'This house and mill built by Jane, the widow of Tho Deane Esqr in ye year 1710.' Bere Mill was the location where young Henry Portal, having secured its lease in 1712 started his company making high quality paper. Demand was such that by 1718, he could move to a larger mill further upstream at Laverstoke, where in 1727 he successfully negotiated a deal with a friend's uncle to supply banknote paper to the Bank of England, a contract that proved so agreeable to both parties that it has continued uninterrupted to this day.

10. Follow the tarmac drive to the right and across the bridge. A little way further on - particularly in spring when the daffodils are out – there's a little stream running parallel to the road here which gives this route a touch of fairy glen about it, but it's a nice walk whatever the season. As the view ahead opens up, the long building over to your left is Whitchurch's former workhouse. Smaller and a lot less severe than most workhouses, and benefiting considerably from its rather more attractive title of 'The Gables'.

11. Continue along the track all the way to the main road alongside the old chalk pit. Turn left for a few yards and then turn down the drive towards the Gables where you will find a footpath on your right that runs

parallel to the road just before the gate.

12. Follow this path to the end and stay on this side of London Road until you see a small path leading uphill over on the right hand side – just before the Prince Regent. This little path takes us along the top of the cliffs carved out of the chalk during the 1800's when the area below was filled with the thatched sheds of a whiting factory, where chalk was ground and washed for use in the manufacture of distemper, putty and clay pipes. There are some good views along here over the rooftops of the village.

13. Eventually you will come to a fork in the path alongside a flint wall. Take the right fork and then shortly afterwards turn right where paths cross by the lamppost to take the path uphill flanked either side by railway sleepers beneath the long-established rookery. The unusual flint bridge we pass under is known locally as 'The Jerusalem Arch' and carried a private pathway through the extensive grounds of Berehill House - once a large and gracious home belonging to the Portal family – now an old peoples home tucking in amongst modern developments and set for demolition at the time of writing. The depth markings on the walls beside the path are interesting, but I have no idea why they're there!

14. When you reach the end of the path, turn left down to the main road and then left down the hill to the town square. From here, we proceed along Bell Street, under the disused railway bridge taking the footpath on the left opposite Bloswood Drive. Cross the stile on the left and follow the well-defined footpath diagonally across the field towards the embankment. This footpath would originally have led you up to the old Great Western railway station on top of the embankment and although the railway line is long gone, the station building still stands and is now a private residence.

15. Go through the kissing gate, and then – alongside the underpass – cross the stile on your right. Follow this path to the left along the edge of the field, skirting to the right of the garages. Then follow the gravelled driveway alongside the cemetery, which will bring you to the B3400 main road.

16. Turn right along the B3400, past the cemetery gate and under the A34 trunk road. Stay on the right hand side, picking up the path by the wall just after the entrance to Hurstbourne Park.

17. Where this footpath emerges from the trees alongside a bench, we are directly opposite the next track we need to follow.

However as this is a rather blind bend on a busy road, please don't try to cross here, proceed a further 100 yards or so down to the 'S' bend sign and cross there.

18. In spring and summer, this little track should be called rabbit alley as you are guaranteed to send at least half a dozen prime specimens bounding off in to the hedgerows with your arrival. Go straight down the track and across the stile at the foot of the slope. Continue along the footpath over a small footbridge (dry every time I've been here) and over the next stile. Here you'll find some old abandoned watercress beds – though left to its own devices the watercress still seemed to be doing fine. Cross the stile and then proceed diagonally across the field to the left towards the embankment. Past some flattened marker posts until you find yet another stile. Follow the path along the foot of the embankment and after another stile or two, you'll find yourself once more on the bank of the River Test.

19. Turn left under the old railway viaduct and then keep to the right where you'll shortly find a stile and a narrow footbridge across the river. Over the bridge, we come into the tiny hamlet of Tufton. Follow the path straight up the bank and turn left along the track towards the town centre. Just round the corner past the barns, the lovely little church of St Mary's is well worth a visit. Inside little seems to have changed over the centuries and on the north wall are the remains of a large painting of St Christopher, said to be almost 800 years old.

20. Just past the church, turn left before the red telephone box – something of a rare sight these days. Follow the gravel drive 100 yards then take the stile over to the right of the big wooden gate. Follow the footpath around the edge of the field, then once at the road turn left under the bridge and then left again into the small field. The footpath runs parallel to the road for a few yards before crossing the field diagonally to the far right corner where you will find a stile. The unusual route is a legacy of the days before the A34T when the diagonal part of this path led straight towards Tufton Manor House.

21. Over the stile, turn left and staying on the left, follow the road back towards Whitchurch. Just past the 40mph signs, take the footpath on the left through the kissing gates and directly across Millennium Green to the wooden fence over on the other side. Make sure you stop for a while to enjoy the wonderful fish bench!

Walk No. 30

22. Continuing along our path, cross straight over when you come to a road and take the narrow footpath over the river and past the Fulling Mill. At mills such as this one, Fullers would scour woollen cloth to remove excess grease and oil before pounding it with hammers driven by the mill in a solution containing Fullers Earth. This would matt together the loose fibres and produce felt. What happened next after the cloth was hung out to dry on special hooks known as tenters, well you'll have to buy my next book to find out! In the 1950's the Fulling Mill briefly became the home of the actor James Robertson Justice, but a tragic family accident at the Mill has meant his stay in the village is only quietly recalled. On the other side of the footbridge, follow the path alongside the river towards the spire of All Hallows church.

23. Turning left at the bench, follow the track up to and across the road to visit All Hallows Church, which has so many interesting features it would be impossible to list them all here. The church has an excellent guidebook usually available within, so I'll just say don't miss it, particularly the moving epitaph written by poor Fanny Blair on her wall plaque in the ringing chamber of the tower. Outside the church, we turn right on our final stretch back towards Whitchurch centre and the end of our walk. The house known as 'The Lawn' which we pass on our right was the home of Lord Denning – former Master of the Rolls and undoubtedly Whitchurch's most famous son.